Comeback Power: Book of Inspiration

Ray

Published by Ray, 2024.

COMEBACK POWER: BOOK OF INSPIRATION

First edition. July 22, 2024.

ISBN: 979-8227474094

Written by Ray.

Table of Contents

DISCLAIMER

This workbook contains quotes and wisdom from various sources. The author of this workbook does not claim authorship or ownership of these original quotes. Every effort has been made to properly attribute these quotes to their respective authors. If any attribution is incorrect or missing, please contact the publisher for correction in future editions.

The content of this workbook, including exercises, reflections, and strategies, has been developed by [Your Name] based on personal experience, research, and inspiration from various sources. However, the interpretation, application, and presentation of ideas stemming from the quoted material are original to this work.

Readers are encouraged to seek out the original works of the quoted authors for a fuller understanding of their ideas and contexts.

The author and publisher have made every effort to ensure the accuracy and completeness of information contained in this book. However, we assume no responsibility for errors, inaccuracies, omissions, or any inconsistency herein.

Introduction: Navigating the Path to Empowerment

Welcome to a transformative exploration of personal growth, resilience, and empowerment. In a world that is constantly evolving and presenting us with both opportunities and challenges, it is essential to equip ourselves with the tools and wisdom needed to navigate our journeys effectively. This book is designed to be your companion on this journey, offering insights, reflections, and practical advice to help you unlock your true potential.

Our lives are a series of moments and decisions, each contributing to the narrative of who we are and who we are becoming. The choices we make, the actions we take, and the mindset we cultivate shape our paths and define our experiences. This book delves into the essence of these elements, exploring themes such as resilience, vision, purpose, relationships, and personal responsibility.

Each chapter is crafted to provide a deep dive into key aspects of personal and professional growth. From understanding the importance of embracing new beginnings to cultivating resilience and harnessing the power of relationships, the insights shared are designed to inspire and guide you in your quest for a fulfilling and impactful life.

We begin by exploring the concept of action and the importance of not just setting intentions but following through with purposeful steps. Carl Jung's assertion that "You are what you do, not what you say you'll do" serves as a cornerstone for this discussion, emphasizing the need for action in shaping our realities. Through practical examples and motivational quotes, we will examine how to transform vision into reality and embrace the power of decisive action.

As we progress, we delve into the themes of personal growth and self-reflection, highlighting the importance of understanding ourselves and our motivations. By reflecting on quotes from thought leaders and philosophers, we uncover the profound impact of self-awareness and inner peace on our journey toward fulfillment.

We will also explore the significance of relationships and the role they play in our lives. The wisdom of iconic characters and real-life figures sheds light on the value of authentic connections and the importance of nurturing meaningful bonds. Through these insights, we learn how to build and maintain relationships that enhance our lives and contribute to our personal growth.

In addition, we address the concept of purpose and passion, emphasizing the need to align our actions with what we truly care about. By examining the interplay between vision and execution, we uncover strategies for turning our dreams into reality and living a life that reflects our deepest values.

Throughout this book, you will find a blend of inspirational quotes, practical advice, and thought-provoking reflections. Each chapter is designed to offer valuable insights and actionable strategies that you can apply to your own life. The goal is not only to inspire but also to equip you with the tools needed to navigate the complexities of life with confidence and clarity.

As you embark on this journey, remember that the path to empowerment is a continuous process of learning, growing, and evolving. Embrace the challenges and opportunities that come your way, and let the lessons from this book serve as a guide on your journey toward a more fulfilling and impactful life.

Thank you for joining me on this exploration of personal and professional growth. Together, let us navigate the path to empowerment and uncover the greatness that lies within each of us.

Chapter 1: The Power of Resilience

"The comeback is always stronger than the setback"

The main quote encapsulates the essence of resilience and the human capacity to overcome adversity. This powerful statement reminds us that our ability to bounce back from challenges is not just equal to, but greater than the obstacles we face. It suggests that setbacks, while difficult, serve as catalysts for growth and improvement. When we experience a setback, we often gain new perspectives, learn valuable lessons, and develop stronger coping mechanisms. These experiences contribute to our personal growth, making our eventual comeback more impactful and meaningful. The word "always" in this quote is particularly significant, as it implies that this principle holds true regardless of the nature or magnitude of the setback. It offers hope and encouragement, reminding us that no matter how dire our circumstances may seem, we have the innate ability to not just recover, but to emerge stronger than before.

"Fall seven times, stand up eight." - Japanese Proverb

The supporting quotes further reinforce this message of resilience. The Japanese proverb beautifully illustrates the persistence required in the face of repeated failures. It suggests that true strength lies not in avoiding falls, but in the determination to rise one more time than we fall. This proverb encourages us to view setbacks not as endpoints, but as stepping stones on our journey to success. Vince Lombardi's quote, "It's not whether you get knocked down, it's whether you get up," echoes this sentiment. It shifts our focus from the inevitability of challenges to our response to them. Lombardi, known for his inspirational leadership in American football, understood that setbacks are a part of any worthwhile endeavor. His words remind us that our character and ultimate success are determined not by the absence of failures, but by our courage and determination in the face of them.

The greatest glory in living lies not in never falling, but in rising every time we fall." - Nelson Mandela

Nelson Mandela's quote, "The greatest glory in living lies not in never falling, but in rising every time we fall," adds another layer to this theme. Coming from a man who endured 27 years of imprisonment before rising to become a symbol of freedom and reconciliation, these words carry profound weight. Mandela's perspective encourages us to see our struggles not as shameful or weakening experiences, but as opportunities for demonstrating our resilience and achieving true glory. It suggests that a life without falls is not only unrealistic but perhaps less meaningful than one marked by persistent rising in the face of adversity. Finally, Lionel Messi's statement, "What defines us is how well we rise after falling," brings this concept into the realm of personal identity. Messi, one of the greatest football players of all time, has faced numerous setbacks in his career, from health issues in his youth to crushing defeats on the world stage. His words remind us that our response to failure is a crucial part of our character. It's not our successes alone that define us, but our ability to maintain our dignity, determination, and spirit in the face of disappointments.

Together, these quotes paint a comprehensive picture of resilience. They remind us that setbacks are not just inevitable, but integral to our personal growth and ultimate success. They encourage us to shift our perspective from viewing falls as failures to seeing them as opportunities for demonstrating our strength and character. These words of wisdom teach us that true resilience isn't about avoiding difficulty, but about cultivating the inner strength to face challenges head-on, learn from our experiences, and continually strive to better ourselves. They remind us that each setback carries within it the seed of a greater comeback, and that our ability to nurture that seed – to rise, to persist, to maintain hope in the face of adversity – is what truly defines us and leads us to our greatest achievements. In essence, these quotes serve as a powerful reminder that our greatest strengths often emerge from our deepest struggles, and that the path to success is paved not with unbroken victory, but with persistent resilience in the face of setbacks.

Chapter 2: Embracing Failure as Opportunity

Failure is the opportunity to begin again more intelligently." - Henry Ford

Henry Ford's profound statement, "Failure is the opportunity to begin again more intelligently," encapsulates a transformative perspective on failure that can revolutionize our approach to challenges and setbacks. This quote invites us to view failure not as an end point, but as a crucial part of the learning process. Ford, a pioneer in the automotive industry who faced numerous setbacks before achieving success, understood that each failure contains valuable lessons. By framing failure as an opportunity, Ford encourages us to approach our attempts with a growth mindset, always seeking to learn and improve. The word "intelligently" is key here, suggesting that we should not simply persist blindly, but rather analyze our failures, extract insights, and apply this new knowledge to our future endeavors. This perspective transforms failure from a source of discouragement to a catalyst for growth and innovation.

The secret of life is to fall seven times and to get up eight times." - Paulo Coelho

Paulo Coelho's quote, "The secret of life is to fall seven times and to get up eight times," beautifully complements Ford's idea. It emphasizes the importance of persistence in the face of repeated failures. Coelho, known for his inspirational writings, suggests that life's true secret lies not in avoiding falls, but in our relentless determination to rise again. This quote normalizes failure as a part of life's journey and celebrates the resilience required to keep moving forward. It reminds us that success often comes not to those who never fail, but to those who refuse to stay down when they do.

Success is not final, failure is not fatal: it is the courage to continue that counts." - Winston Churchill

Winston Churchill's words, "Success is not final, failure is not fatal: it is the courage to continue that counts," add another layer to this theme. Churchill, who led Britain through the darkest days of World War II, understood deeply the transient nature of both success and failure. His quote reminds us that neither success nor failure is a permanent state. Instead, what truly matters is our courage and determination to persist in the face of challenges. This perspective can be incredibly liberating, freeing us from the fear of failure and the complacency of success, and encouraging us to focus on the ongoing journey of growth and achievement.

"I can't change the direction of the wind, but I can adjust my sails to always reach my destination." - Jimmy Dean

Jimmy Dean's quote, "I can't change the direction of the wind, but I can adjust my sails to always reach my destination," introduces the concept of adaptability in the face of unchangeable circumstances. This metaphor beautifully illustrates that while we can't control every aspect of our environment or situation, we have the power to adjust our approach and attitude. Dean's words encourage us to focus on what we can control - our responses and strategies - rather than becoming discouraged by factors beyond our influence. This adaptability is a crucial component of turning failures into opportunities, allowing us to navigate around obstacles and find new paths to our goals.

"It's hard to beat a person who never gives up." - Babe Ruth

Finally, Babe Ruth's statement, "It's hard to beat a person who never gives up," underscores the power of persistence. Ruth, one of baseball's greatest players, was known not just for his home runs but also for his strikeouts. His quote reminds us that ultimate success often belongs not to those who never fail, but to those who refuse to be defeated by failure. It suggests that persistence itself is a formidable strength, capable of overcoming a multitude of setbacks and challenges.

Collectively, these quotes paint a picture of failure as a natural and even necessary part of the journey to success. They encourage us to reframe our understanding of failure, seeing it not as a reflection of our worth or abilities, but as a valuable tool for learning and growth. This perspective allows us to approach our goals with greater resilience and adaptability. Instead of being paralyzed by the fear of failure, we can embrace it as an opportunity to gain new insights, refine our strategies, and ultimately become more effective in our pursuits.

Moreover, these quotes highlight the importance of persistence and courage in the face of setbacks. They remind us that success is rarely a linear path, but rather a journey marked by ups and downs. By maintaining our determination and willingness to learn from each experience, we can turn our failures into stepping stones toward our goals. This mindset not only increases our chances of ultimate success but also allows us to find value and growth in every part of our journey, regardless of the immediate outcome.

In essence, these quotes teach us that embracing failure as an opportunity is not about celebrating our mistakes, but about recognizing the potential for growth and improvement inherent in every setback. They encourage us to approach our endeavors with a combination of intelligence, adaptability, courage, and unwavering persistence. By doing so, we can transform our failures into powerful catalysts for personal and professional growth, ultimately leading us to greater achievements than we might have imagined possible.

Chapter 3: Overcoming Self-Doubt

"The only limit to our realization of tomorrow will be our doubts of today." - Franklin D. Roosevelt

Franklin D. Roosevelt's powerful statement, "The only limit to our realization of tomorrow will be our doubts of today," encapsulates the profound impact that self-doubt can have on our potential and achievements. This quote, coming from a leader who guided the United States through the Great Depression and World War II while battling his own physical limitations, carries immense weight. It suggests that our doubts, more than any external obstacles, are what truly hold us back from realizing our full potential. Roosevelt's words invite us to examine our self-imposed limitations and question whether they are based on reality or merely on our fears and insecurities. By framing doubt as the primary barrier to our future success, this quote empowers us to take control of our destiny by first conquering our internal struggles.

Strength doesn't come from what you can do. It comes from overcoming the things you once thought you couldn't." - Rikki Rogers

Rikki Rogers' quote, "Strength doesn't come from what you can do. It comes from overcoming the things you once thought you couldn't," beautifully complements

Chapter 3

Roosevelt's idea. It redefines the concept of strength, suggesting that true power lies not in our innate abilities, but in our capacity to surpass our perceived limitations. This perspective is particularly encouraging because it implies that strength is not a fixed trait, but something we can actively develop by challenging ourselves and pushing beyond our comfort zones. Rogers' words remind us that each time we overcome something we once thought impossible, we not only achieve that specific goal but also build our overall resilience and self-confidence.

You may encounter many defeats, but you must not be defeated." - Maya Angelou

Maya Angelou's quote, "You may encounter many defeats, but you must not be defeated," adds another layer to this theme of overcoming self-doubt. Angelou, a renowned poet and civil rights activist who overcame numerous personal and societal obstacles, understood the difference between experiencing setbacks and allowing those setbacks to define us. Her words encourage us to maintain our sense of self and our determination even in the face of repeated challenges. This quote suggests that defeat is not something that happens to us externally, but a state of mind that we have the power to reject. It reminds us that our response to adversity is far more important than the adversity itself.

"The phoenix must burn to emerge." - Janet Fitch

Janet Fitch's metaphorical statement, "The phoenix must burn to emerge," introduces the concept of transformation through adversity. The phoenix, a mythical bird that rises from its own ashes, serves as a powerful symbol of renewal and rebirth. Fitch's words suggest that sometimes we must go through painful or challenging experiences to emerge stronger and more resilient. This perspective can be particularly comforting when facing difficult times, as it reframes these experiences not as mere suffering, but as necessary steps in our personal growth and transformation. It encourages us to embrace our challenges, knowing that they have the potential to forge us into stronger, more capable versions of ourselves.

"Rock bottom became the solid foundation on which I rebuilt my life." - J.K. Rowling

J.K. Rowling's deeply personal quote, "Rock bottom became the solid foundation on which I rebuilt my life," provides a real-world example of overcoming extreme self-doubt and adversity. Rowling, who wrote the first Harry Potter book while struggling as a single mother on welfare, understands firsthand the power of resilience in the face of seemingly insurmountable odds. Her words remind us that even our lowest points can serve as the bedrock for future success. This quote encourages us to view our struggles not as endpoints, but as starting points for rebuilding and reimagining our lives. It suggests that there's nowhere to go but up when we've hit rock bottom, providing hope and motivation to those facing their own personal nadirs.

Together, these quotes form a powerful narrative about the nature of self-doubt and our ability to overcome it. They remind us that doubt is a natural part of the human experience, but it need not define or limit us. Instead, by confronting our doubts head-on, we can transform them into opportunities for growth and self-discovery. These words of wisdom encourage us to reframe our perceptions of strength, failure, and adversity. They suggest that true strength lies not in avoiding challenges or doubt, but in our ability to persist and grow despite them.

Moreover, these quotes highlight the transformative power of overcoming self-doubt. They remind us that each time we push past our perceived limitations, we not only achieve our immediate goal but also expand our sense of what's possible. This expanded self-belief can have a compounding effect, enabling us to take on greater challenges and achieve even more significant successes in the future.

The quotes also emphasize the importance of resilience and perseverance in the face of setbacks. They encourage us to maintain our sense of self and our determination, even when facing repeated defeats. By doing so, we can transform our challenges into opportunities for growth and renewal, emerging stronger and more capable than before.

In essence, these quotes teach us that overcoming self-doubt is not about eliminating uncertainty or fear from our lives. Rather, it's about developing the courage and resilience to pursue our goals despite these feelings. They remind us that our doubts are not facts, but merely thoughts that we have the power to challenge and overcome. By embracing this mindset, we can unlock our full potential and achieve things we once thought impossible. Whether we're facing personal struggles, professional challenges, or societal obstacles, these words of wisdom provide encouragement and guidance, reminding us of our innate strength and our capacity for growth and transformation.

Chapter 4: The Strength Within

"You never know how strong you are until being strong is your only choice." - Bob Marley

Bob Marley's profound statement, "You never know how strong you are until being strong is your only choice," encapsulates a fundamental truth about human resilience and inner strength. This quote, coming from a man who faced numerous hardships throughout his life, including poverty, political violence, and ultimately a battle with cancer, carries significant weight. It suggests that our true strength often remains hidden until we are faced with situations that demand its emergence. Marley's words remind us that we often possess reserves of strength far beyond what we imagine, reserves that only reveal themselves in times of great need or adversity. This perspective can be incredibly empowering, as it suggests that we are capable of handling far more than we might believe under normal circumstances.

"Sometimes you don't realize your own strength until you come face to face with your greatest weakness." - Susan Gale

Susan Gale's quote, "Sometimes you don't realize your own strength until you come face to face with your greatest weakness," adds a nuanced layer to Marley's idea. It suggests that our moments of greatest vulnerability or perceived weakness can actually be catalysts for discovering our true strength. This paradoxical concept encourages us to embrace our weaknesses and challenges, rather than fear or avoid them, as they may be the very experiences that reveal our hidden capabilities. Gale's words remind us that strength and weakness are not opposites, but interconnected aspects of our character that can inform and enhance each other.

"The harder you fall, the higher you bounce." - Doug Horton

Doug Horton's statement, "The harder you fall, the higher you bounce," introduces an optimistic perspective on setbacks and failures. This metaphorical expression suggests that the magnitude of our struggles can directly correlate with the intensity of our comeback. It encourages us to view our falls not as defeats, but as springboards for greater achievements. Horton's words remind us that resilience isn't just about getting back to where we were before a setback, but about using the energy of that setback to propel us even further than we were before. This perspective can transform our approach to challenges, helping us see them as opportunities for dramatic growth and improvement rather than as obstacles to be feared.

"Resilience is knowing that you are the only one that has the power and the responsibility to pick yourself up." - Mary Holloway

Mary Holloway's quote, "Resilience is knowing that you are the only one that has the power and the responsibility to pick yourself up," emphasizes the personal nature of resilience. It reminds us that while we may receive support and encouragement from others, ultimately, the power to recover and move forward lies within ourselves. This perspective is both empowering and sobering, as it places the responsibility for our resilience squarely on our own shoulders. Holloway's words encourage us to take ownership of our recovery process, reminding us that we have both the capability and the obligation to lift ourselves up in times of adversity.

"When you come to the end of your rope, tie a knot and hang on." - Franklin D. Roosevelt

Franklin D. Roosevelt's advice, "When you come to the end of your rope, tie a knot and hang on," provides a practical metaphor for perseverance in the face of seemingly insurmountable odds. Coming from a leader who guided his nation through some of its darkest hours while dealing with his own physical limitations, these words carry particular resonance. The image of tying a knot at the end of one's rope suggests resourcefulness and determination in the face of limited options. It encourages us to find creative solutions and to persist even when we feel we've exhausted all our resources. Roosevelt's quote reminds us that often, holding on just a little longer can make all the difference in overcoming our challenges.

Collectively, these quotes paint a comprehensive picture of inner strength and resilience. They remind us that our capacity for endurance and recovery is often far greater than we realize, and that this capacity is revealed and developed through our confrontations with adversity. These words of wisdom encourage us to view challenges not as insurmountable obstacles, but as opportunities to discover and cultivate our inner strength.

Moreover, these quotes highlight the personal nature of resilience. While external support can be valuable, they remind us that true strength comes from within and that we each have the power and responsibility to nurture our own resilience. This perspective can be incredibly empowering, as it places the control over our responses to adversity firmly in our own hands.

The quotes also emphasize the transformative power of resilience. They suggest that by facing our challenges head-on and persevering through difficult times, we not only overcome our immediate obstacles but also grow stronger and more capable in the process. This growth can enable us to reach heights we might never have achieved without facing and overcoming adversity.

In essence, these quotes teach us that inner strength is not a fixed trait, but a capacity that can be developed and expanded through our experiences with adversity. They encourage us to embrace our challenges, to persist in the face of setbacks, and to trust in our ability to recover and grow stronger. Whether we're facing personal struggles, professional obstacles, or societal challenges, these words of wisdom provide encouragement and guidance. They remind us of our innate resilience and our capacity not just to endure, but to thrive in the face of adversity. By embracing this mindset, we can unlock reservoirs of strength we never knew we possessed, enabling us to overcome challenges and achieve things we once thought impossible.

Chapter 5: The Power of Will

The difference between a successful person and others is not a lack of strength, not a lack of knowledge, but rather a lack in will." - Vince Lombardi

Vince Lombardi's powerful statement, "The difference between a successful person and others is not a lack of strength, not a lack of knowledge, but rather a lack in will," cuts to the core of what truly drives achievement. Lombardi, renowned for his success as an American football coach, understood that willpower is the critical factor that separates those who achieve their goals from those who fall short. This quote suggests that while strength and knowledge are important, they are ultimately insufficient without the determination to put them into action. It emphasizes that success is not merely about having capabilities, but about having the resolve to fully utilize those capabilities in pursuit of our goals. Lombardi's words serve as a reminder that our will – our determination, perseverance, and commitment – is the engine that drives us toward success, even in the face of obstacles and setbacks.

"Life is not about waiting for the storms to pass. It's about learning how to dance in the rain." - Vivian Greene

Vivian Greene's quote, "Life is not about waiting for the storms to pass. It's about learning how to dance in the rain," beautifully complements Lombardi's emphasis on willpower. This metaphorical expression encourages us to embrace life's challenges rather than passively waiting for better circumstances. The image of dancing in the rain suggests finding joy and purpose even in difficult times, highlighting the role of attitude and perspective in our ability to persevere. Greene's words remind us that life will always have its storms, and true resilience lies not in avoiding these challenges, but in learning to thrive despite them. This quote emphasizes the power of will in shaping our experiences and finding positivity even in adversity.

"It's not the failure that holds us back but the reluctance to begin over again that causes us to stagnate." - Clarissa Pinkola Estés

Clarissa Pinkola Estés' insight, "It's not the failure that holds us back but the reluctance to begin over again that causes us to stagnate," adds another dimension to the concept of willpower. Estés, a Jungian psychoanalyst and author, points out that failure itself is not the primary obstacle to success; rather, it's our hesitation to try again after experiencing failure that truly impedes our progress. This quote underscores the importance of resilience and the will to persist in the face of setbacks. It suggests that our ability to bounce back and start anew is a crucial component of success, highlighting the role of willpower in overcoming the psychological barriers that failure can create.

"Tough times never last, but tough people do." - Robert H. Schuller

Robert H. Schuller's statement, "Tough times never last, but tough people do," offers a concise and powerful reminder of the enduring nature of human resilience. Schuller, a motivational speaker and author, emphasizes that while difficulties are temporary, the strength of character developed through facing these challenges is lasting. This quote encourages us to focus on building our inner toughness – our will – rather than being overwhelmed by the transient nature of our problems. It reminds us that by cultivating a strong will, we can outlast any hardship we face.

"The oak fought the wind and was broken, the willow bent when it must and survived." - Robert Jordan

Robert Jordan's metaphorical quote, "The oak fought the wind and was broken, the willow bent when it must and survived," introduces the concept of adaptability as a crucial aspect of willpower. This imagery, drawn from Jordan's fantasy novels, illustrates that true strength often lies not in rigid resistance, but in the flexibility to adapt to changing circumstances. The oak tree, despite its apparent strength, breaks under pressure, while the seemingly weaker willow survives by bending with the wind. This metaphor suggests that willpower isn't just about brute force or unyielding determination, but also about the wisdom to know when to stand firm and when to yield and adapt.

Together, these quotes paint a comprehensive picture of the power of will and its crucial role in achieving success and overcoming adversity. They remind us that willpower is not just about raw determination, but encompasses a range of qualities including persistence, adaptability, resilience, and the ability to maintain a positive outlook in the face of challenges.

These words of wisdom emphasize that success is largely a product of our mindset and our willingness to persevere. They suggest that while we cannot control all of life's circumstances, we have significant power over how we respond to those circumstances. By cultivating a strong will, we can learn to "dance in the rain," to begin again after failure, to outlast tough times, and to adapt flexibly to challenges.

Moreover, these quotes highlight the transformative nature of willpower. They imply that by exercising our will – by choosing to persist, to adapt, to try again – we not only overcome immediate obstacles but also build our character and expand our capabilities. This growth in turn enhances our ability to face future challenges, creating a virtuous cycle of resilience and achievement.

The quotes also remind us that willpower is not about never falling or never facing difficulty. Rather, it's about how we respond to these inevitable aspects of life. They encourage us to view challenges not as insurmountable barriers, but as opportunities for growth and self-discovery.

In essence, these quotes teach us that the power of will is a fundamental driver of success and personal growth. They encourage us to cultivate our willpower, to persist in the face of adversity, to adapt to changing circumstances, and to maintain a positive outlook even in difficult times. Whether we're pursuing personal goals, professional ambitions, or navigating life's challenges, these words of wisdom provide guidance and inspiration. They remind us that with a strong will, we have the power to shape our experiences, overcome obstacles, and achieve things we might once have thought impossible. By embracing this mindset, we can unlock our full potential and lead more resilient, fulfilling lives.

Chapter 6: Mastering Your Mind

"You have power over your mind – not outside events. Realize this, and you will find strength." - Marcus Aurelius

Marcus Aurelius's profound statement, "You have power over your mind – not outside events. Realize this, and you will find strength," encapsulates a fundamental principle of Stoic philosophy and serves as a powerful reminder of our innate ability to control our thoughts and reactions. This quote, coming from a Roman emperor who faced numerous challenges during his reign, emphasizes the distinction between external circumstances, which are often beyond our control, and our internal responses, which we can govern. Aurelius suggests that true strength and peace come not from attempting to control the uncontrollable, but from mastering our own minds. This perspective can be incredibly empowering, as it shifts our focus from external factors to our internal landscape, where we have the most influence. It reminds us that regardless of what happens around us, we always retain the power to choose our thoughts, attitudes, and responses.

"When we learn how to become resilient, we learn how to embrace the beautifully broad spectrum of the human experience." - Jaeda DeWalt

Jaeda DeWalt's quote, "When we learn how to become resilient, we learn how to embrace the beautifully broad spectrum of the human experience," adds a dimension of richness and depth to the concept of mental mastery. DeWalt suggests that resilience isn't just about enduring hardship, but about fully engaging with the entire range of human experiences – both positive and negative. This perspective encourages us to view challenges not as things to be avoided, but as integral parts of a full and meaningful life. By developing resilience, we open ourselves up to a broader, more nuanced understanding of what it means to be human. This quote reminds us that mastering our mind isn't about eliminating negative experiences, but about developing the capacity to appreciate and learn from all of life's moments.

"No matter how hard the past, you can always begin again."
- Buddha

The Buddha's timeless wisdom, "No matter how hard the past, you can always begin again," offers a message of hope and renewal. This quote emphasizes the power of the present moment and our ability to start fresh, regardless of our history. It suggests that our past experiences, no matter how difficult, do not have to define our future. This perspective is crucial in mastering our minds, as it frees us from the burden of past mistakes or traumas and empowers us to shape our present and future. The Buddha's words remind us that each moment offers an opportunity for a new beginning, encouraging us to let go of what we cannot change and focus on what we can influence in the here and now.

The human capacity for burden is like bamboo – far more flexible than you'd ever believe at first glance." - Jodi Picoult

Jodi Picoult's metaphor, "The human capacity for burden is like bamboo – far more flexible than you'd ever believe at first glance," provides a vivid illustration of our mental resilience. Bamboo is known for its strength and flexibility, able to bend under immense pressure without breaking. By comparing our capacity for burden to bamboo, Picoult suggests that we are far more resilient than we often give ourselves credit for. This perspective encourages us to trust in our ability to adapt and endure, even when faced with seemingly overwhelming challenges. It reminds us that mastering our mind involves recognizing and nurturing our innate strength and flexibility.

We don't develop courage by being happy every day. We develop it by surviving difficult times and challenging adversity." - Barbara De Angelis

Barbara De Angelis's insight, "We don't develop courage by being happy every day. We develop it by surviving difficult times and challenging adversity," highlights the role of adversity in building mental strength. De Angelis suggests that courage, a key aspect of mental mastery, is not developed through constant comfort and ease, but through facing and overcoming challenges. This quote reminds us that difficult experiences, while uncomfortable, are often the most potent catalysts for personal growth and mental fortitude. It encourages us to view adversity not as something to be avoided, but as an opportunity to cultivate courage and resilience.

Collectively, these quotes paint a comprehensive picture of what it means to master one's mind. They remind us that mental mastery is not about controlling external events or eliminating all negative experiences. Rather, it's about developing the capacity to respond to life's varied experiences with resilience, flexibility, and courage.

These words of wisdom emphasize that our power lies in our ability to choose our thoughts and reactions, regardless of external circumstances. They encourage us to embrace the full spectrum of human experience, recognizing that both joy and challenge contribute to our growth and understanding. By doing so, we can develop a more nuanced and resilient approach to life.

Moreover, these quotes highlight the importance of perspective in mastering our minds. They remind us that we have the power to reframe our experiences, to see opportunities for new beginnings, and to recognize our own strength and flexibility. This shift in perspective can be transformative, allowing us to approach life's challenges with greater confidence and equanimity.

The quotes also underline the role of adversity in developing mental strength. They suggest that it's through facing and overcoming difficulties that we truly grow and develop our mental capacities. This perspective can help us approach challenges not with fear or resentment, but with a sense of opportunity for growth and self-discovery.

In essence, these quotes teach us that mastering our mind is an ongoing process of self-awareness, resilience, and growth. They encourage us to cultivate our inner strength, to embrace life's full range of experiences, and to trust in our capacity to adapt and overcome. Whether we're facing personal struggles, professional challenges, or simply navigating the complexities of daily life, these words of wisdom provide guidance and inspiration. They remind us that by mastering our minds – by choosing our thoughts, embracing our experiences, and cultivating our resilience – we can find strength, peace, and fulfillment, regardless of external circumstances. This mastery empowers us to live more intentionally, to respond to life's challenges with greater wisdom and equanimity, and to unlock our full potential for growth and self-realization.

Chapter 7: Shaping Your Destiny

**I am not what happened to me, I am what I choose to become."
- Carl Jung**

Carl Jung's profound statement, "I am not what happened to me, I am what I choose to become," encapsulates the essence of personal empowerment and the human capacity for self-determination. This quote, coming from one of the founders of modern psychology, emphasizes the distinction between our experiences and our identity. Jung suggests that while our past events and circumstances undoubtedly influence us, they do not define us. Instead, our true identity is shaped by our conscious choices and the direction we decide to take in life. This perspective is incredibly empowering as it places the responsibility and power for shaping our destiny squarely in our own hands. It encourages us to move beyond a victim mentality and to embrace our role as the architects of our own lives.

"It's your reaction to adversity, not adversity itself that determines how your life's story will develop." - Dieter F. Uchtdorf

Dieter F. Uchtdorf's quote, "It's your reaction to adversity, not adversity itself that determines how your life's story will develop," beautifully complements Jung's idea. Uchtdorf, a religious leader and former airline executive, highlights the crucial role our responses play in shaping our life's trajectory. This quote reminds us that while we cannot always control the challenges we face, we have complete control over how we react to them. It suggests that our destiny is not determined by the adversities we encounter, but by the way we choose to interpret and respond to these experiences.

This perspective encourages us to focus on developing resilience and a positive mindset, as these are the tools that will ultimately shape our life's story.

You've got to be able to hold a lot of contradictory ideas in your mind without going nuts. I feel like to be successful, you have to be able to be both ahead of your time and behind it." - George Carlin

George Carlin's insight, "You've got to be able to hold a lot of contradictory ideas in your mind without going nuts. I feel like to be successful, you have to be able to be both ahead of your time and behind it," introduces the concept of cognitive flexibility as a key component in shaping our destiny. Carlin, known for his incisive social commentary, suggests that success in life often requires the ability to navigate complexity and embrace paradox. This quote encourages us to move beyond black-and-white thinking and to develop the mental agility to hold multiple, even contradictory, perspectives simultaneously. It reminds us that shaping our destiny often involves balancing tradition and innovation, stability and change, caution and risk-taking.

"Life doesn't get easier or more forgiving, we get stronger and more resilient." - Steve Maraboli

Steve Maraboli's statement, "Life doesn't get easier or more forgiving, we get stronger and more resilient," offers a powerful perspective on personal growth and development. Maraboli, a behavioral scientist and author, suggests that the key to navigating life's challenges lies not in hoping for easier circumstances, but in developing our internal resources. This quote encourages us to focus on building our strength and resilience rather than wishing for a more forgiving world. It reminds us that by embracing challenges and using them as opportunities for growth, we can continuously expand our capacity to shape our destiny, regardless of external circumstances.

"Resilience is accepting your new reality, even if it's less good than the one you had before." - Elizabeth Edwards

Elizabeth Edwards' definition, "Resilience is accepting your new reality, even if it's less good than the one you had before," adds a nuanced understanding of what it means to shape our destiny. Edwards, who faced numerous personal tragedies, emphasizes that resilience and personal growth sometimes involve accepting and adapting to new realities that may be less desirable than our previous circumstances. This perspective reminds us that shaping our destiny isn't always about achieving an idealized vision, but sometimes about finding meaning and purpose within the constraints of our current reality. It encourages us to cultivate flexibility and acceptance as key tools in navigating life's unexpected turns.

Collectively, these quotes paint a comprehensive picture of what it means to shape one's destiny. They remind us that our power to influence our life's direction lies not in controlling external events, but in choosing our responses, developing our inner resources, and cultivating mental flexibility and resilience.

These words of wisdom emphasize that shaping our destiny is an active, ongoing process. They encourage us to take responsibility for our lives, to view challenges as opportunities for growth, and to continuously develop our mental and emotional capacities. By doing so, we can navigate life's complexities with greater skill and intentionality.

Moreover, these quotes highlight the importance of mindset in shaping our destiny. They suggest that our beliefs about ourselves and our abilities play a crucial role in determining our life's trajectory. By cultivating a growth mindset and believing in our capacity for change and development, we open ourselves up to new possibilities and opportunities.

The quotes also underline the role of resilience and adaptability in shaping our destiny. They remind us that life often involves unexpected turns and setbacks, and that our ability to bounce back, learn from these experiences, and adapt to new realities is crucial in determining our long-term outcomes.

In essence, these quotes teach us that shaping our destiny is about more than just setting goals or making plans. It's about developing the inner resources, mental flexibility, and resilience to navigate life's complexities and challenges. They encourage us to take an active role in our personal growth, to embrace challenges as opportunities for development, and to cultivate a mindset that allows us to learn and adapt continuously.

Whether we're facing personal crossroads, professional challenges, or simply trying to live more intentionally, these words of wisdom provide guidance and inspiration. They remind us that while we cannot control every aspect of our lives, we have significant power to shape our destiny through our choices, attitudes, and responses. By embracing this perspective, we can approach life with greater confidence, purpose, and agency, ultimately creating a destiny that aligns with our deepest values and aspirations.

Chapter 8: Learning from Adversity

"The gem cannot be polished without friction, nor man perfected without trials." - Chinese Proverb

The Chinese proverb, "The gem cannot be polished without friction, nor man perfected without trials," encapsulates a profound truth about the role of adversity in personal growth and development. This timeless wisdom draws a parallel between the physical process of refining a gemstone and the metaphorical process of human character development. Just as a rough gem requires friction and pressure to reveal its true beauty and value, the proverb suggests that human beings need to face challenges and difficulties to reach their full potential. This perspective encourages us to view adversity not as a mere obstacle or misfortune, but as a necessary and valuable part of our personal evolution. It reminds us that the difficulties we face are often the very experiences that shape us, strengthen us, and bring out our best qualities.

The bamboo that bends is stronger than the oak that resists." - Japanese Proverb

The Japanese proverb, "The bamboo that bends is stronger than the oak that resists," offers a complementary perspective on dealing with adversity. This saying uses natural imagery to illustrate the power of flexibility and adaptability in the face of challenges. While the oak tree might seem stronger due to its rigid structure, it's more likely to break under extreme pressure. In contrast, the bamboo's ability to bend allows it to withstand even strong winds without breaking. This metaphor encourages us to cultivate resilience and adaptability rather than rigid resistance when facing life's storms. It suggests that true strength often lies in our ability to be flexible, to adapt to changing circumstances, and to bounce back from setbacks.

"Adversity is like a strong wind. It tears away from us all but the things that cannot be torn, so that we see ourselves as we really are." - Arthur Golden

Arthur Golden's insight, "Adversity is like a strong wind. It tears away from us all but the things that cannot be torn, so that we see ourselves as we really are," provides a poignant description of how adversity can reveal our true nature. Golden, author of "Memoirs of a Geisha," suggests that challenging times strip away our pretenses and superficial concerns, leaving only our core values and true character. This perspective encourages us to view adversity as a clarifying force, one that helps us understand what truly matters to us and what we're genuinely made of. It reminds us that while adversity can be painful, it also offers a unique opportunity for self-discovery and authenticity.

"The world breaks everyone, and afterward, some are strong at the broken places." - Ernest Hemingway

Ernest Hemingway's observation, "The world breaks everyone, and afterward, some are strong at the broken places," offers a nuanced view of how we can grow through adversity. Hemingway, known for his terse yet profound writing style, acknowledges the universal nature of suffering while highlighting the potential for growth that comes from it. This quote suggests that while adversity may 'break' us in some ways, it also creates opportunities for us to rebuild ourselves stronger than before. It's a reminder that our wounds and struggles, when properly healed and integrated, can become sources of unique strength and resilience.

In the middle of difficulty lies opportunity." - Albert Einstein

Albert Einstein's statement, "In the middle of difficulty lies opportunity," provides an optimistic and proactive approach to adversity. Einstein, one of the most influential scientists of the 20th century, encourages us to look for the hidden opportunities within our challenges. This perspective shifts our focus from the negative aspects of difficult situations to the potential positive outcomes or lessons they might offer. It reminds us that adversity often forces us to think creatively, to push our boundaries, and to discover new solutions or paths forward that we might not have considered otherwise.

Collectively, these quotes paint a comprehensive picture of the role of adversity in personal growth and development. They remind us that challenges and difficulties, while often uncomfortable or painful, are essential components of our journey towards becoming our best selves.

These words of wisdom emphasize that adversity is not just something to be endured, but a powerful catalyst for growth, self-discovery, and transformation. They encourage us to shift our perspective on difficult times, viewing them not as mere obstacles to be overcome, but as opportunities for learning, strengthening, and refining our character.

Moreover, these quotes highlight the importance of our response to adversity. They suggest that while we cannot always control the challenges we face, we have significant power over how we interpret and react to these experiences. By choosing to approach adversity with flexibility, openness, and a growth mindset, we can maximize its potential for positive transformation in our lives.

The quotes also underline the universality of adversity. They remind us that everyone faces challenges and difficulties, but it's our response to these trials that ultimately shapes our character and determines our path forward.

In essence, these quotes teach us that learning from adversity is a crucial aspect of personal development and success. They encourage us to embrace challenges as opportunities for growth, to remain flexible and adaptable in the face of difficulties, and to look for the lessons and opportunities hidden within our struggles.

Whether we're facing personal setbacks, professional challenges, or global crises, these words of wisdom provide guidance and inspiration. They remind us that by approaching adversity with the right mindset, we can not only survive our challenges but use them as stepping stones to become stronger, wiser, and more resilient versions of ourselves. This perspective empowers us to face life's difficulties with courage and optimism, knowing that each challenge we overcome contributes to our personal growth and helps us unlock our full potential.

Chapter 9: Building Character Through Challenges

"Character cannot be developed in ease and quiet. Only through experience of trial and suffering can the soul be strengthened, ambition inspired, and success achieved." - Helen Keller

Helen Keller's profound statement, "Character cannot be developed in ease and quiet. Only through experience of trial and suffering can the soul be strengthened, ambition inspired, and success achieved," encapsulates the essential role of challenges in building character. Keller, who overcame the extraordinary challenges of being deaf and blind to become a renowned author and activist, speaks from a place of deep personal experience. Her words remind us that true strength of character is not innate, but forged through adversity. This quote suggests that it is precisely our struggles and difficulties that provide the necessary conditions for personal growth and development. Keller's perspective encourages us to view challenges not as obstacles to be avoided, but as crucial opportunities for strengthening our resolve, inspiring our ambitions, and ultimately achieving success.

"The greatest test of courage on earth is to bear defeat without losing heart." - Robert Green Ingersoll

Robert Green Ingersoll's insight, "The greatest test of courage on earth is to bear defeat without losing heart," highlights a specific aspect of character building through challenges. Ingersoll, a 19th-century orator and political leader, points to the importance of resilience in the face of failure or defeat. This quote suggests that true courage is not just about facing challenges head-on, but about maintaining hope and determination even when we don't succeed. It reminds us that how we handle our defeats is often more revealing of our character than how we handle our victories. This perspective encourages us to view setbacks not as final judgments on our worth or abilities, but as temporary obstacles that we can overcome with persistent effort and unwavering spirit.

"Courage doesn't always roar. Sometimes courage is the little voice at the end of the day that says I'll try again tomorrow." - Mary Anne Radmacher

Mary Anne Radmacher's quote, "Courage doesn't always roar. Sometimes courage is the little voice at the end of the day that says I'll try again tomorrow," offers a nuanced understanding of what courage looks like in everyday life. Radmacher, a writer and artist, reminds us that courage is not always about grand gestures or dramatic actions. Often, it's about the quiet persistence that keeps us going in the face of repeated challenges or disappointments. This perspective is particularly valuable when building character through long-term challenges, where progress may be slow and setbacks frequent. It encourages us to recognize and value the small acts of courage that sustain us day after day.

"Persistence and resilience only come from having been given the chance to work through difficult problems." - Gever Tulley

Gever Tulley's observation, "Persistence and resilience only come from having been given the chance to work through difficult problems," underscores the importance of facing challenges directly in order to build character. Tulley, an education innovator, suggests that we can only develop true persistence and resilience by actually engaging with and working through difficulties. This quote reminds us that while we might instinctively want to shield ourselves or others from challenges, doing so can actually hinder character development. It encourages us to embrace difficult problems as opportunities for growth, knowing that each challenge we overcome contributes to our overall resilience and ability to persist in the face of future obstacles.

"Resilience is very different than being numb. Resilience means you experience, you feel, you fail, you hurt. You fall. But, you keep going." - Yasmin Mogahed

Yasmin Mogahed's insight, "Resilience is very different than being numb. Resilience means you experience, you feel, you fail, you hurt. You fall. But, you keep going," provides a powerful description of what true resilience looks like. Mogahed, an author and spiritual teacher, emphasizes that resilience is not about becoming hardened or insensitive to difficulties. Instead, it's about fully experiencing our challenges and setbacks, acknowledging the pain and disappointment they may bring, but choosing to continue forward despite these feelings. This perspective encourages us to approach character building not as a process of becoming invulnerable to hardship, but as a journey of learning how to move forward even while acknowledging and processing our difficulties.

Collectively, these quotes paint a comprehensive picture of how challenges contribute to building character. They remind us that character development is not a passive process, but an active engagement with life's difficulties and setbacks.

These words of wisdom emphasize that true character is revealed and strengthened through how we respond to challenges.

They encourage us to view difficulties not as unfortunate accidents or unfair burdens, but as essential components of our personal growth and development.

Moreover, these quotes highlight the multifaceted nature of character building through challenges. They suggest that this process involves developing courage, persistence, resilience, and the ability to maintain hope and determination even in the face of setbacks or failures.

The quotes also underline the importance of actually engaging with challenges rather than avoiding them. They remind us that while facing difficulties can be uncomfortable or painful, it is through this direct engagement that we develop the strength of character that will serve us throughout our lives.

In essence, these quotes teach us that building character through challenges is a fundamental aspect of personal growth and success. They encourage us to embrace difficulties as opportunities for development, to persist in the face of setbacks, and to recognize the value of both dramatic acts of courage and quiet, everyday persistence.

Whether we're facing personal obstacles, professional challenges, or societal issues, these words of wisdom provide guidance and inspiration. They remind us that by approaching challenges with the right mindset, we can use them as tools for building a stronger, more resilient character. This perspective empowers us to face life's difficulties with courage and determination, knowing that each challenge we overcome contributes to our personal growth and helps us become the best versions of ourselves.

Chapter 10: Taking Action

In this chapter, "Taking Action," we delve into the heart of progress: action. The words we speak may hold potential, but it is our actions that truly define us. The essence of this chapter is captured in Carl Gustav Jung's profound quote, "You are what you do, not what you say you'll do." This simple yet powerful statement emphasizes that our identity and legacy are forged not by our intentions or promises but by the tangible actions we take. Alongside Jung's quote, we'll explore sub-quotes from Ryder Carroll, Robert Frost, Babe Ruth, and T. Harv Eker, each offering a unique perspective on the importance of action in overcoming obstacles and achieving success.

"You are what you do, not what you say you'll do." - Carl Gustav Jung

Carl Gustav Jung's quote underscores the importance of action over words. In a world where declarations and promises are often made lightly, Jung reminds us that it is what we do that truly matters. Our actions are the true reflection of our character, intentions, and values. Words can be powerful, but without action, they remain empty and unfulfilled. This quote challenges us to align our actions with our words, ensuring that our deeds speak louder than our promises. It calls for integrity and accountability, urging us to be doers rather than mere talkers. By living out our commitments, we become authentic and reliable, building trust and respect in our relationships and endeavors.

"No matter how bleak or menacing a situation may appear, it does not entirely own us. It can't take away

our freedom to respond, our power to take action." - Ryder Carroll

Ryder Carroll's quote highlights the concept of agency and resilience. Regardless of the difficulties we face, we retain the power to choose our response. Circumstances may be dire, but they do not dictate our actions. This perspective empowers us to reclaim control, even in the most challenging situations. By recognizing that our power to act remains intact, we can navigate adversity with determination and hope. This quote encourages us to look beyond the immediate obstacles and focus on our ability to influence outcomes through our choices and actions. It is a reminder that we are never truly powerless as long as we can take action.

"The best way out is always through." - Robert Frost

Robert Frost's quote speaks to the necessity of perseverance. When faced with challenges, the instinct may be to avoid or circumvent them, but Frost suggests that confronting obstacles head-on is the most effective approach. By facing our difficulties directly, we gain strength, wisdom, and resilience. This process may be arduous, but it leads to genuine progress and resolution. Frost's words remind us that avoidance only prolongs our struggles, whereas taking action to address our problems can lead to meaningful breakthroughs and growth. This quote encourages us to embrace the journey through our challenges, trusting that each step forward brings us closer to our goals.

"Every strike brings me closer to the next home run." - Babe Ruth

Babe Ruth's quote is a testament to the power of persistence and positive thinking. In baseball, as in life, failure is inevitable, but it is also a stepping stone to success. Each "strike" or failure is not a setback but a learning opportunity that brings us closer to our ultimate goal. Ruth's perspective transforms failure from a source of discouragement to a catalyst for progress. This mindset fosters resilience, encouraging us to keep pushing forward despite setbacks. By viewing each failure as a step towards success, we maintain motivation and optimism, which are crucial for sustained effort and eventual achievement. Ruth's quote is a powerful reminder that persistence in the face of failure is essential for reaching our aspirations.

"How you do anything is how you do everything." - T. Harv Eker

T. Harv Eker's quote emphasizes the importance of consistency and integrity in our actions. It suggests that our approach to small tasks reflects our overall attitude and approach to life. Attention to detail, dedication, and effort in minor activities translate to our larger goals and endeavors. This principle encourages us to cultivate good habits and a strong work ethic in all areas of our lives, as these qualities will permeate everything we do. Eker's quote challenges us to bring our best selves to every task, no matter how insignificant it may seem, recognizing that excellence in the small things builds a foundation for excellence in the big things. This consistency is key to achieving long-term success and fulfillment.

Together, these quotes weave a powerful narrative about the importance of action in overcoming challenges and achieving success. Jung's assertion that we are defined by our actions sets the stage for understanding the profound impact of what we do. Carroll's emphasis on our freedom to respond empowers us to take control of our circumstances, no matter how daunting. Frost's insight on facing challenges head-on reinforces the necessity of perseverance. Ruth's perspective on failure as a step towards success inspires resilience and optimism. Finally, Eker's call for consistency reminds us that our habits and attitudes in small tasks reflect our overall approach to life and success.

In "Taking Action," we explore how these principles can be applied in practical ways to transform intentions into achievements. By embodying the wisdom of these quotes, we can navigate life's challenges with determination, resilience, and integrity, ultimately becoming the best versions of ourselves through our actions.

Chapter 11: Embracing New Beginnings

In "Embracing New Beginnings," we explore the transformative power of change and resilience. The main quote by Alexander Graham Bell, "When one door closes, another opens; but we often look so long and so regretfully upon the closed door that we do not see the one which has opened for us," serves as the central theme of this chapter. It highlights the importance of moving forward and recognizing new opportunities that arise, even in the face of loss or disappointment. Complementing Bell's insight, we delve into sub-quotes from Kahlil Gibran, Bram Stoker, Confucius, and Will Smith, each offering profound perspectives on resilience, hope, and the strength to embrace new beginnings.

"When one door closes, another opens; but we often look so long and so regretfully upon the closed door that we do not see the one which has opened for us." - Alexander Graham Bell

Alexander Graham Bell's quote encapsulates the essence of new beginnings. It reminds us that endings are not definitive; they pave the way for new opportunities. However, our focus on what we've lost can blind us to these new possibilities. By dwelling on closed doors, we miss the chance to walk through open ones. This quote encourages a shift in perspective, urging us to embrace change and remain open to new paths. It is a call to let go of regrets and to have the courage to explore new horizons, trusting that each end is a precursor to a fresh start.

"Out of suffering have emerged the strongest souls; the most massive characters are seared with scars." - Kahlil Gibran

Kahlil Gibran's quote speaks to the strength and resilience forged through adversity. Suffering, though painful, often shapes us into stronger individuals. The scars we bear are testament to our survival and growth. This perspective transforms suffering from a source of despair into a crucible for personal development. Gibran's words inspire us to view our hardships as opportunities to build character and resilience. By embracing the scars of our past, we recognize our capacity to endure and emerge stronger, ready to face new beginnings with a fortified spirit.

"It is really wonderful how much resilience there is in human nature. Let any obstructing cause, no matter what, be removed in any way, even by death, and we fly back to first principles of hope and enjoyment." - Bram Stoker

Bram Stoker's quote highlights the inherent resilience of the human spirit. No matter the obstacle, once it is removed, our natural inclination is to return to hope and joy. This resilience is a fundamental aspect of our nature, enabling us to recover from even the most devastating losses. Stoker's words reassure us that our capacity for hope and enjoyment is enduring, even in the face of significant challenges. This quote encourages us to trust in our innate ability to rebound and to look forward to the new beginnings that follow the removal of any impediment.

"Our greatest glory is not in never falling, but in rising every time we fall." - Confucius

Confucius's quote emphasizes the importance of perseverance and resilience. True glory lies not in avoiding failure, but in our ability to rise each time we fall. This perspective shifts the focus from the inevitability of setbacks to the strength and determination required to overcome them. It encourages us to view failures as temporary and surmountable, reinforcing the idea that each fall is an opportunity to rise again. Confucius's words inspire us to embrace new beginnings with the confidence that we can recover and grow from every fall.

"Those that say I can and those that say I can't are both usually right." - Will Smith and Confucius

This quote, attributed to both Will Smith and Confucius, highlights the power of mindset in shaping our reality. Our beliefs about our capabilities often determine our success or failure. Those who believe they can achieve something are likely to find ways to do so, while those who doubt themselves are likely to fall short. This quote underscores the importance of a positive and empowering mindset when facing new beginnings. It encourages us to adopt a "can-do" attitude, recognizing that our beliefs play a crucial role in our ability to seize new opportunities and overcome challenges.

Together, these quotes weave a narrative of resilience, hope, and the courage to embrace new beginnings. Bell's insight into the opportunities that follow endings sets the stage for a discussion on the transformative power of change. Gibran's acknowledgment of the strength derived from suffering reinforces the idea that adversity can be a catalyst for growth. Stoker's affirmation of human resilience highlights our inherent ability to return to hope and joy, even after significant losses. Confucius's emphasis on rising after falls reminds us that perseverance is key to navigating new beginnings. Finally, the combined wisdom of Will Smith and Confucius on the power of mindset encourages us to believe in our ability to succeed.

In "Embracing New Beginnings," we explore how these principles can be applied to navigate the transitions in our lives. By shifting our focus from closed doors to open ones, cultivating resilience through adversity, trusting in our natural ability to rebound, embracing the inevitability of setbacks, and adopting a positive mindset, we can face new beginnings with confidence and optimism. This chapter invites us to let go of past regrets, embrace change, and trust in our capacity to create a brighter future through our actions and attitudes.

Chapter 12: Cultivating Resilience

In "Cultivating Resilience," we delve into the strength and persistence required to overcome adversity. The main quote by Nelson Mandela, "The greatest glory in living lies not in never falling, but in rising every time we fall," embodies the essence of resilience, emphasizing that true success and glory come from our ability to recover from setbacks. This chapter is supported by insights from Mary Holloway, Jodi Picoult, Steve Maraboli, and a Japanese proverb, each shedding light on different facets of resilience and our capacity to bounce back stronger from life's challenges.

"The greatest glory in living lies not in never falling, but in rising every time we fall." - Nelson Mandela

Nelson Mandela's quote serves as the cornerstone of this chapter, underscoring that falling is an inevitable part of life, but our response to these falls defines our character and success. Mandela, who faced immense personal and political hardships, knew firsthand the power of resilience. His words inspire us to view each fall not as a failure but as an opportunity to demonstrate our strength and determination. Rising after a fall requires courage, perseverance, and an unwavering belief in our ability to overcome obstacles. This quote encourages us to embrace our falls, learn from them, and rise with renewed vigor and wisdom.

"Resilience is knowing that you are the only one that has the power and the responsibility to pick yourself up." - Mary Holloway

Mary Holloway's quote emphasizes personal responsibility in cultivating resilience. It highlights the empowering realization that we hold the key to our recovery. This perspective encourages self-reliance and accountability, reminding us that while external support can be valuable, the ultimate power to rise lies within us. Holloway's words inspire us to take ownership of our journey, to trust in our ability to navigate challenges, and to actively engage in the process of rebuilding and moving forward. By acknowledging our responsibility, we become more proactive and resilient in the face of adversity.

"The human capacity for burden is like bamboo – far more flexible than you'd ever believe at first glance." - Jodi Picoult

Jodi Picoult's comparison of human resilience to bamboo illustrates the surprising strength and flexibility we possess. Bamboo, though appearing delicate, bends without breaking, symbolizing how we can endure and adapt to pressure and adversity. This metaphor highlights that our initial perceptions of our limitations are often far from reality. Picoult's words encourage us to recognize and trust in our hidden reserves of strength and flexibility. By embracing our capacity to bend and adapt, we become more resilient, able to withstand and recover from the pressures and challenges we face.

"Life doesn't get easier or more forgiving, we get stronger and more resilient." - Steve Maraboli

Steve Maraboli's quote reframes the challenges of life as catalysts for personal growth. It suggests that rather than waiting for life to become easier, we should focus on becoming stronger and more resilient. This perspective empowers us to view hardships as opportunities to build our inner strength and resilience. Maraboli's words inspire a proactive approach to personal development, encouraging us to continually enhance our ability to cope with and overcome challenges. By embracing this mindset, we shift our focus from external circumstances to our internal growth, becoming more resilient and capable individuals.

"The bamboo that bends is stronger than the oak that resists." - Japanese Proverb

The Japanese proverb about bamboo and oak underscores the strength found in flexibility and adaptability. While the oak tree may seem stronger due to its rigidity, it is the bamboo that survives storms by bending with the wind. This wisdom teaches us that resilience is not about being unyielding but about adapting to circumstances without breaking. Flexibility allows us to navigate and survive life's storms, emerging stronger and more resilient. The proverb encourages us to cultivate a mindset of adaptability, understanding that our ability to bend and adjust is a crucial aspect of resilience.

Together, these quotes offer a comprehensive exploration of resilience, each adding depth and nuance to our understanding of this essential trait. Mandela's focus on rising after each fall sets the stage for a discussion on the nature of resilience. Holloway's emphasis on personal responsibility reminds us that the power to overcome lies within us. Picoult's metaphor of bamboo illustrates our surprising strength and flexibility, while Maraboli's perspective on growth through adversity encourages a proactive approach to personal development. The Japanese proverb reinforces the value of adaptability, highlighting the strength found in bending rather than breaking.

In "Cultivating Resilience," we explore how these principles can be applied to build and strengthen our resilience. By accepting that falls are a part of life, taking responsibility for our recovery, recognizing our hidden strengths, focusing on personal growth, and embracing flexibility, we can navigate challenges with greater confidence and effectiveness. This chapter invites us to embrace our inherent resilience, to trust in our ability to rise after every fall, and to view each challenge as an opportunity to grow and become stronger. Through these practices, we cultivate a resilient spirit capable of thriving in the face of adversity.

Chapter 13: The Hero's Journey

In "The Hero's Journey," we explore the transformation from ordinary to extraordinary, the moral dilemmas faced by heroes, and the ultimate realization of what it means to be a true hero. The main quote by Harvey Dent, "You either die a hero or live to become a villain," encapsulates the duality and complexity of heroism, highlighting the thin line between hero and villain. This chapter is enriched by quotes from iconic characters like Batman, Tony Stark, and Ra's Al Ghul, each offering unique insights into the essence of heroism, the importance of actions over identity, and the pursuit of ideals.

"You either die a hero or live to become a villain." - Harvey Dent

Harvey Dent's quote from "The Dark Knight" serves as a profound reflection on the nature of heroism and morality. It suggests that a hero's journey is fraught with the danger of becoming corrupted by the very forces they seek to combat. This quote emphasizes the precarious balance heroes must maintain, where prolonged exposure to power and adversity can lead to moral compromise. It invites us to consider the internal and external challenges that can transform a hero into a villain, underscoring the importance of vigilance and integrity in maintaining one's heroic ideals.

"It's not who I am underneath, but what I do that defines me." – Batman: Dark Knight Trilogy

Batman's quote highlights the primacy of actions over identity in defining heroism. It suggests that our deeds, rather than our intentions or hidden selves, are what truly matter. This perspective shifts the focus from internal motivations to external impacts, encouraging us to judge ourselves and others based on actions. Batman's words inspire us to take responsibility for our choices and their consequences, reinforcing the idea that true heroism is demonstrated through consistent, positive actions, regardless of one's internal struggles or personal identity.

"I shouldn't be alive, unless it was for a reason. I know what I have to do, and I know it is right." - Tony Stark, Iron Man

Tony Stark's quote from "Iron Man" speaks to the sense of purpose that drives a hero. Surviving a life-threatening experience, Stark realizes that his survival must have a greater meaning, propelling him to take action for the greater good. This quote highlights the transformative power of near-death experiences in redefining one's purpose and direction. Stark's words remind us that discovering and embracing our purpose can give us the strength and clarity to act decisively and ethically, even in the face of overwhelming challenges.

"If you become more than a man, devote yourself to an ideal, then you become something else entirely." - Ra's Al Ghul, Batman Begins

Ra's Al Ghul's quote from "Batman Begins" delves into the transformative potential of devotion to an ideal. By transcending personal limitations and embodying an ideal, one can become a symbol of hope, justice, or other virtues. This perspective suggests that true heroism involves self-transcendence, where personal desires and limitations are subsumed by a larger cause. Ra's Al Ghul's words inspire us to aspire beyond our individual selves, to commit to ideals that can elevate our actions and influence, transforming us into symbols of those ideals.

"If you are nothing without the suit, then you shouldn't have it." - Tony Stark, Spider-Man: Homecoming

Tony Stark's advice to Spider-Man in "Spider-Man: Homecoming" emphasizes the importance of inner strength and character over external tools or powers. It suggests that true heroism is rooted in one's intrinsic qualities rather than in external enhancements. This quote serves as a reminder that relying too heavily on external symbols of power can undermine our self-worth and effectiveness. Stark's words encourage us to cultivate our inner virtues and capabilities, ensuring that our heroism is grounded in who we are, not what we possess.

Together, these quotes provide a multi-faceted exploration of the hero's journey, each highlighting different aspects of what it means to be a hero. Harvey Dent's reflection on the duality of heroism sets the stage for examining the moral complexities and potential pitfalls of the heroic path. Batman's emphasis on actions over identity reinforces the importance of deeds in defining heroism, while Tony Stark's realization of purpose underscores the motivational power of discovering one's calling. Ra's Al Ghul's perspective on devotion to ideals elevates the discussion to the realm of self-transcendence, and Stark's advice about intrinsic worth highlights the need for inner strength and character.

In "The Hero's Journey," we explore how these principles can be applied to our own lives, guiding us in our pursuit of heroism. By maintaining vigilance against moral corruption, prioritizing our actions, discovering and embracing our purpose, committing to higher ideals, and cultivating our inner virtues, we can navigate our own heroic journeys with integrity and resilience. This chapter invites us to reflect on our own paths, to identify the ideals that inspire us, and to take decisive, ethical actions that define our heroism. Through these practices, we can aspire to become true heroes in our own right, embodying the values and ideals that we hold dear.

Chapter 14: The Value of Time and Life

In "The Value of Time and Life," we delve into the profound importance of time and the quality of life, reflecting on how our perspectives, choices, and actions shape our existence. The main quote by Tony Stark, "No amount of money ever bought a second of time," encapsulates the irreplaceable nature of time, highlighting that wealth cannot compensate for lost moments. This chapter is further enriched by insights from characters in "John Wick: Chapter 4" and the timeless wisdom of Marcus Aurelius, each offering a unique perspective on living a meaningful life.

"No amount of money ever bought a second of time." - Tony Stark, Avengers: Endgame

Tony Stark's quote from "Avengers: Endgame" emphasizes the irreplaceable nature of time, a resource that remains constant and finite for everyone, regardless of wealth or status. This statement highlights the futility of materialism when it comes to extending our lifespan. It serves as a poignant reminder to value and make the most of the time we have, investing it in meaningful pursuits and relationships rather than chasing financial gain. Stark's reflection encourages us to prioritize experiences, connections, and personal growth, recognizing that time, once lost, cannot be regained.

"A Good Death Only Comes After A Good Life." - Shimazu, John Wick: Chapter 4 (2023)

Shimazu's quote from "John Wick: Chapter 4" presents the idea that a well-lived life is a prerequisite for a good death. It suggests that the way we live our lives—our choices, actions, and relationships—determines the quality and peace of our final moments. This perspective invites us to lead lives of integrity, purpose, and fulfillment, ensuring that when our time comes, we can look back without regret. It emphasizes the importance of living each day with intention and striving to leave a positive legacy.

"Those Who Cling To Death; Live." - Caine, John Wick: Chapter 4 (2023)

Caine's quote from "John Wick: Chapter 4" offers a paradoxical view on life and death. It suggests that an acute awareness of mortality can enhance our appreciation for life, prompting us to live more fully and authentically. By acknowledging and accepting the inevitability of death, we may be inspired to seize opportunities, take risks, and live with greater passion and purpose. Caine's words encourage us to embrace the present moment, understanding that the fleeting nature of life can motivate us to make the most of every day.

"Those Who Have Something To Live For, Those Who Have Something To Die For, And Those Who Have Something To Kill For." - Marquis, John Wick: Chapter 4 (2023)

Marquis's quote from "John Wick: Chapter 4" explores the different motivations that drive individuals. It highlights that having a clear purpose—whether it's something to live for, die for, or even fight for—can give our lives direction and meaning. This statement underscores the importance of finding and committing to our personal values and causes. It prompts us to reflect on what matters most to us and how these priorities shape our actions and decisions, ultimately defining the quality and significance of our lives.

"The happiness of your life depends on the quality of your thoughts." - Marcus Aurelius

Marcus Aurelius's quote from his "Meditations" underscores the profound impact of our thoughts on our overall well-being and happiness. This Stoic principle suggests that our inner dialogue and mindset shape our experiences and perceptions of life. By cultivating positive, rational, and constructive thoughts, we can enhance our emotional resilience, find contentment, and navigate challenges more effectively. Aurelius's wisdom encourages us to practice mindfulness and self-awareness, recognizing that our mental state is a powerful determinant of our quality of life.

Together, these quotes provide a comprehensive exploration of the value of time and life, each offering a distinct yet interconnected perspective. Tony Stark's reflection on the irreplaceable nature of time sets the foundation, reminding us to cherish and wisely use our limited time. Shimazu's emphasis on living a good life to ensure a good death aligns with this, urging us to make each moment count. Caine's paradoxical insight into the life-enhancing awareness of death encourages us to live more fully, while Marquis's exploration of motivations highlights the importance of purpose in giving our lives direction. Finally, Marcus Aurelius's focus on the quality of our thoughts ties these themes together, underscoring the role of our mindset in shaping our experiences and happiness.

In "The Value of Time and Life," we are invited to reflect deeply on how we spend our time and the legacy we wish to leave behind. By prioritizing meaningful pursuits, cultivating a positive mindset, and living with purpose and integrity, we can enhance the quality of our lives. This chapter challenges us to reevaluate our priorities, embrace the present moment, and make conscious choices that align with our values and aspirations. Through these practices, we can ensure that our time is spent in ways that enrich our lives and the lives of those around us, creating a fulfilling and impactful existence.

Chapter 15: The Power of Relationships

In "The Power of Relationships," we explore the deep and transformative impact that relationships have on our lives. The connections we form with others can provide support, love, and strength, shaping our experiences and helping us navigate through life's challenges. The main quote from Deadpool, "These people in this picture are my entire world," captures the essence of how relationships can become the cornerstone of our existence. This chapter delves into the significance of these bonds through various quotes from iconic characters, each offering a unique perspective on the importance of relationships.

"These people in this picture are my entire world." - Deadpool

Deadpool's quote underscores the profound importance of the people we cherish in our lives. This statement highlights how our closest relationships can become our entire world, providing us with love, purpose, and a sense of belonging. For Deadpool, the people in his picture represent his core support system, the ones he fights for and draws strength from. This quote reminds us that the connections we forge with others are not just a part of our lives; they can become the very foundation of our existence, influencing our actions, decisions, and overall well-being.

"I am with you until the end of the line." - Steve Rogers

Steve Rogers' quote from "Captain America: The Winter Soldier" exemplifies unwavering loyalty and friendship. This powerful declaration of commitment to his friend Bucky Barnes highlights the importance of standing by those we care about, especially during difficult times. It emphasizes that true friendship is characterized by steadfast support and dedication, no matter the circumstances. Steve's words inspire us to be reliable and faithful companions, reinforcing the idea that enduring relationships are built on mutual trust and loyalty.

"I love you in every universe." - Dr. Strange

Dr. Strange's quote from "Doctor Strange in the Multiverse of Madness" expresses the timeless and boundless nature of love. It suggests that genuine love transcends time, space, and even different realities. This profound statement reminds us that the depth of our connections can endure beyond any physical or temporal boundaries. It encourages us to appreciate and nurture the love we share with others, recognizing its infinite potential to bring meaning and fulfillment to our lives.

"Staying together is more important than how we stay together." - Black Widow

Black Widow's quote from "Avengers: Endgame" highlights the significance of unity and togetherness, especially in the face of adversity. It suggests that the strength of a relationship lies in the commitment to stay together, regardless of the challenges that may arise. This perspective emphasizes the importance of prioritizing the bond itself over the specifics of how it is maintained. It encourages us to focus on the bigger picture and the enduring value of being there for each other, even when circumstances are tough.

"Friendship means nothing when it's convenient." - Shimazu

Shimazu's quote from "John Wick: Chapter 4" underscores the idea that true friendship is not based on convenience but on genuine connection and support. It suggests that real friends stand by each other through thick and thin, even when it is difficult or inconvenient. This statement challenges us to evaluate the authenticity of our relationships, urging us to be dependable and supportive friends, especially when it matters most. It reminds us that the true test of friendship is how we act during challenging times, not just when it is easy.

Together, these quotes provide a comprehensive exploration of the power and significance of relationships. Deadpool's reflection on the central role of loved ones in his life sets the foundation, emphasizing that our relationships can become our entire world. Steve Rogers' commitment to loyalty, Dr. Strange's expression of timeless love, Black Widow's focus on unity, and Shimazu's challenge to be a true friend all contribute to a deeper understanding of what it means to form and maintain meaningful connections.

In "The Power of Relationships," we are invited to reflect on the people who matter most to us and the impact they have on our lives. By valuing loyalty, nurturing love, prioritizing unity, and committing to being dependable friends, we can cultivate relationships that provide support, joy, and strength. This chapter encourages us to invest time and effort into our connections, recognizing that the bonds we form with others are among the most valuable and enduring aspects of our lives. Through these relationships, we find the resilience and inspiration to face life's challenges, knowing that we are not alone and that we are supported by those who care about us deeply.

Chapter 16: Vision and Execution

Vision and execution are two sides of the same coin when it comes to achieving success. A clear and compelling vision sets the direction, but without execution, it remains a mere dream. The main quote, "Vision without execution is just hallucination," emphasizes the crucial need to translate ideas into action. This chapter delves into the importance of combining vision with effective execution through various perspectives from notable figures, highlighting how ideas are only powerful when they are implemented.

"Vision without execution is just hallucination."-Thomas Edison

This quote succinctly captures the essence of the relationship between vision and execution. A vision, no matter how grand or inspiring, is useless without the actions to realize it. Execution turns dreams into reality, and without it, visions are merely fantasies—hallucinations of what could be. This quote serves as a reminder that successful outcomes depend not just on what we imagine, but on what we do.

"I don't have inspiration, I only have ideas and deadlines." - Stan Lee

Stan Lee's pragmatic approach to creativity emphasizes the importance of discipline and action over waiting for inspiration. Lee, the legendary creator of numerous beloved comic book characters, knew that ideas were only valuable when they were acted upon within set timeframes. This quote highlights the necessity of deadlines and structured work to bring creative visions to life. It suggests that execution is driven by commitment and the practical application of ideas, rather than waiting for the perfect moment of inspiration.

"It doesn't matter who we are, what matters is our plan."-Bane

This quote underscores the significance of having a clear, actionable plan. It suggests that identity and status are secondary to having a strategic approach. Whether in business, personal development, or any other area, what truly matters is the ability to devise and follow through on a plan. This perspective reinforces the idea that success is not about who you are but about what you do with your ideas and how effectively you implement them.

"The genius thing that we did was, we didn't give up." - Jay-Z

Jay-Z's quote speaks to the power of perseverance in execution. Often, the difference between success and failure is the willingness to keep going despite obstacles and setbacks. This statement highlights that persistence and resilience are crucial components of execution. It's not just about having a vision but also about the determination to see it through to the end, even when the journey is tough. Jay-Z's success story is a testament to the importance of relentless effort in achieving one's goals.

"Good things come to those that wait, it comes early to those that hustle while they wait." - Thomas Edison

Thomas Edison's quote illustrates the value of proactive effort. While patience is important, it is the active pursuit of goals during the waiting period that accelerates success. Edison, known for his numerous inventions, believed in the power of hard work and continuous effort. This quote encourages a balance between patience and hustle, emphasizing that taking action while waiting for results can lead to quicker and more significant achievements.

Together, these quotes provide a multifaceted view of the relationship between vision and execution. The main quote by itself sets the foundation, stressing that vision without execution is ineffective. Stan Lee's focus on ideas and deadlines, the emphasis on planning, Jay-Z's celebration of perseverance, and Edison's call to hustle all contribute to a comprehensive understanding of what it takes to turn vision into reality.

In "Vision and Execution," we explore the dynamic interplay between dreaming big and taking concrete steps to achieve those dreams. Vision provides direction and inspiration, but it is the actions we take, the plans we make, and the persistence we show that bring those visions to life. This chapter encourages readers to not only dream but to act, to plan meticulously, and to persevere through challenges. By combining vision with execution, we can transform our ideas from mere hallucinations into tangible successes, achieving greatness through our commitment to action.

Chapter 17: Personal Growth and Self-Reflection

Personal growth and self-reflection are essential components of leading a fulfilling and meaningful life. The main quote, "We never lose our demons, Mordo. We only learn to live above them," from The Ancient One in *Doctor Strange*, captures the essence of this journey. It emphasizes that personal growth is not about eliminating our inner struggles but rather about rising above them. This chapter explores how acknowledging and understanding our flaws, mistakes, and limitations can lead to profound self-improvement and resilience.

"We never lose our demons, Mordo. We only learn to live above them." - The Ancient One, Doctor Strange

This quote highlights a fundamental truth about personal growth: our inner demons, such as fears, doubts, and insecurities, do not disappear. Instead, personal growth involves learning to rise above these challenges. By accepting and understanding our demons, we can navigate life with greater wisdom and strength. This perspective encourages self-reflection and the acknowledgment that growth is a continuous process of overcoming our internal struggles.

"I make grave mistakes all the time. Everything seems to work out." - Thor Odinson, Thor: Ragnarok (2017)

Thor's acknowledgment of his mistakes and the realization that things still work out is a powerful lesson in resilience and self-acceptance. This quote reminds us that making mistakes is a natural part of life and personal growth. Instead of being paralyzed by the fear of failure, embracing our errors as opportunities for learning and growth can lead to positive outcomes. Thor's experience encourages us to view our mistakes as stepping stones rather than obstacles.

"Prison is not concrete walls or iron bars. Self-doubt, limitation, and fear are a much better prison." - Grandma Mattie

Grandma Mattie's wisdom reveals that the most restrictive prisons are not physical but mental. Self-doubt, limitations, and fear can imprison us far more effectively than any physical barrier. This quote urges us to reflect on the ways we limit ourselves and to recognize that true freedom comes from overcoming these internal constraints. By confronting and dismantling these mental barriers, we can achieve greater personal growth and liberation.

"The core of believing is a lie." - Grandma Mattie

This provocative quote challenges us to examine the foundations of our beliefs. It suggests that what we believe may often be built on falsehoods or misconceptions. Personal growth involves questioning and critically evaluating our beliefs to uncover the truths that lie beneath. This process of self-reflection can lead to a deeper understanding of ourselves and the world around us, allowing us to grow and evolve.

"Thought can ruin or make you." - Jim Rohn

Jim Rohn's quote emphasizes the power of our thoughts in shaping our lives. Our mindset and the way we think about ourselves and our circumstances can either empower us or hold us back. Positive, constructive thoughts can lead to personal growth and success, while negative, destructive thoughts can lead to stagnation and failure. This quote encourages us to cultivate a mindset that fosters growth and resilience, recognizing that our thoughts have a profound impact on our lives.

Together, these quotes provide a comprehensive view of personal growth and self-reflection. The main quote by The Ancient One sets the stage, emphasizing the importance of rising above our inner demons. Thor's acknowledgment of mistakes, Grandma Mattie's insights on mental prisons and the nature of belief, and Jim Rohn's focus on the power of thought all contribute to a nuanced understanding of the journey of personal growth.

In "Personal Growth and Self-Reflection," we explore the importance of understanding and embracing our imperfections, questioning our beliefs, and cultivating a positive mindset. This chapter encourages readers to reflect deeply on their inner lives, to accept their flaws, and to use their experiences as opportunities for growth. By learning to live above our demons, embracing our mistakes, and challenging our limiting beliefs, we can achieve profound personal transformation and lead more fulfilling lives.

Chapter 18: Facing Life's Challenges

Life is a series of challenges that test our resolve, strength, and determination. The main quote, "The hardest choices require the strongest wills," spoken by Thanos in *Avengers: Infinity War*, captures the essence of this chapter. It highlights the necessity of inner strength and determination when confronted with difficult decisions. This chapter delves into the complexities of making tough choices and facing life's adversities, drawing on the wisdom of various characters and thought leaders.

"The hardest choices require the strongest wills." - Thanos

Thanos's quote underscores the idea that significant and difficult decisions demand immense inner strength. Whether we agree with his actions or not, the quote speaks to the universal truth that facing life's toughest challenges requires a resolute will and unwavering determination. It's a reminder that in moments of adversity, our strength of character is truly tested.

"Once you have done what you had to, the world will not let you do what you want to." - Catwoman

Catwoman's quote reflects the often harsh reality that fulfilling one's duties and obligations can sometimes restrict personal freedom and desire. It emphasizes the sacrifice and discipline required to face life's challenges. This quote encourages readers to understand that while responsibilities may limit immediate gratification, they are essential steps in overcoming obstacles and achieving long-term goals.

"If people treat you like an option, leave them like a choice." - Joker

The Joker's quote speaks to the importance of self-respect and assertiveness in the face of life's interpersonal challenges. It suggests that allowing oneself to be treated as an option by others undermines one's value. By choosing to walk away from such situations, one asserts their worth and integrity. This quote inspires readers to prioritize their self-worth and to make choices that reflect their dignity.

"He's out of line but he's right." - Falcon

Falcon's quote acknowledges the uncomfortable truth that sometimes, the right course of action or the truth itself can be difficult to accept. It underscores the importance of recognizing and confronting uncomfortable truths, even when they challenge our beliefs or actions. This quote encourages readers to be open to criticism and to have the courage to act on what is right, despite the discomfort it may bring.

"Do not take it personally, everyone is glad it is you and not them." - Jim Rohn

Jim Rohn's quote offers a candid perspective on human nature and adversity. It highlights that people often distance themselves from others' challenges, finding relief that they are not in the same situation. This quote advises against taking such reactions personally, instead focusing on one's own strength and resilience. It serves as a reminder to not let others' indifference affect one's resolve in facing challenges.

Together, these quotes provide a comprehensive view of facing life's challenges. Thanos's main quote sets the stage, emphasizing the need for a strong will when making difficult decisions.

Catwoman's insight on duty and sacrifice, the Joker's emphasis on self-respect, Falcon's acknowledgment of uncomfortable truths, and Jim Rohn's perspective on human nature all contribute to a nuanced understanding of resilience and determination.

In "Facing Life's Challenges," we explore the necessity of strength, sacrifice, and self-respect in overcoming adversity. This chapter encourages readers to embrace their inner strength, make tough decisions with confidence, and prioritize their self-worth. By understanding the complexities of duty, recognizing uncomfortable truths, and maintaining resilience in the face of others' indifference, readers can navigate life's challenges with grace and determination. This chapter serves as a guide for cultivating the inner fortitude needed to confront and overcome the obstacles that life inevitably presents.

Chapter 19: Illuminating Your Greatness

Illuminating one's greatness involves discovering and nurturing the unique gifts and purposes that lie within. The main quote, "One minute spent in the Light is enough to show a man how long he has been in the darkness," by Jon Wasson, captures the transformative power of enlightenment and self-realization. This chapter delves into the journey of moving from ignorance to awareness, from darkness to light, and finding one's true purpose and greatness.

"One minute spent in the Light is enough to show a man how long he has been in the darkness." - Jon Wasson

Wasson's quote highlights the profound impact of enlightenment. Even a brief moment of clarity can reveal how long one has been lost in confusion or ignorance. This moment of insight can be life-changing, serving as a catalyst for personal growth and transformation. It emphasizes the importance of seeking knowledge and understanding, as even a short exposure to truth and light can illuminate the path ahead.

"True greatness is found in pursuing the Kingdom more than the day before." - Jon Wasson

This quote underscores the idea that greatness is not a destination but a continuous journey. By striving to improve and grow each day, one moves closer to their true potential and purpose. The "Kingdom" represents one's highest aspirations and spiritual goals. This pursuit requires dedication, perseverance, and a commitment to personal and spiritual growth. Each day's efforts build upon the last, leading to true greatness over time.

"Gift discovery is the fruit of service." - Jon Wasson

Wasson suggests that discovering one's unique talents and gifts often comes through serving others. Service provides opportunities to explore and utilize one's abilities in meaningful ways. By focusing on the needs of others, individuals can uncover their strengths and passions, leading to a deeper understanding of their purpose. This quote highlights the interconnectedness of service and self-discovery, emphasizing that helping others can illuminate one's path to greatness.

"The son of a question is a journey, and the answer is the spirit that guides you." - Jon Wasson

This metaphorical quote illustrates the process of seeking knowledge and understanding. A question initiates a journey of exploration and discovery, with the answer serving as a guiding force throughout this journey. The "spirit" represents intuition, wisdom, and inner guidance that help navigate the complexities of life. By embracing curiosity and the pursuit of answers, one embarks on a transformative journey that reveals deeper truths and insights.

"Your purpose is what provides time its infinite value." - Jon Wasson

Wasson emphasizes that understanding and living one's purpose gives life and time their true value. Without a sense of purpose, time can feel empty and meaningless. However, when one aligns their actions with their purpose, each moment becomes valuable and significant. This quote encourages readers to seek and embrace their purpose, as it brings meaning and fulfillment to their lives, making each moment count.

Together, these quotes offer a comprehensive perspective on illuminating one's greatness. Wasson's main quote sets the stage, emphasizing the transformative power of enlightenment. The sub-quotes then explore the continuous pursuit of personal and spiritual growth, the role of service in discovering one's gifts, the journey of seeking knowledge, and the importance of living a purposeful life.

In "Illuminating Your Greatness," readers are encouraged to seek moments of clarity and enlightenment, recognizing their transformative potential. The chapter emphasizes the continuous journey of self-improvement and the pursuit of higher goals, highlighting the importance of daily dedication to personal and spiritual growth. It also underscores the value of service in discovering one's unique talents and the role of curiosity and exploration in gaining deeper insights. Ultimately, it stresses the significance of living a purposeful life, as this gives true value to each moment and leads to a fulfilling and meaningful existence.

By embracing these principles, readers can illuminate their own greatness, moving from darkness to light and uncovering the true potential within themselves. This chapter serves as a guide for embarking on this journey, offering insights and inspiration for discovering and nurturing one's unique gifts and purpose.

Chapter 21: The Unbreakable Spirit - Perseverance and Determination

In the face of life's countless challenges, setbacks, and obstacles, there exists a powerful force within each of us - the unbreakable spirit of perseverance and determination. This inner strength, when harnessed, can propel us through the toughest of times and elevate us to heights we never thought possible. The journey of life is not always smooth, but it is in navigating its rocky terrain that we truly discover our potential and forge our character.

"I can do this all day" - Captain America

Let's begin with the iconic words of Captain America: "I can do this all day." This simple yet powerful statement encapsulates the essence of perseverance. It's not about how many times you get knocked down; it's about your willingness to get back up, time and time again. Captain America, a symbol of unwavering resolve, reminds us that true strength lies not in never falling, but in rising every time we fall.

This quote speaks to the heart of what it means to be determined. It's about setting your mind to a task or goal and refusing to give up, no matter how difficult the path becomes. It's about facing each new challenge with the same vigor and resolve as the first, even when fatigue sets in and the odds seem insurmountable. This mindset is what separates those who achieve their dreams from those who merely dream.

Consider the moments in your own life when you've faced seemingly insurmountable odds. Perhaps it was a grueling project at work, a personal health challenge, or a long-term goal that seemed to slip further away with each attempt. In those moments, channeling the spirit of "I can do this all day" can be the difference between success and failure. It's about finding that reserve of strength within yourself, that wellspring of determination that refuses to run dry.

"And then I smiled once again not because I was happy but because I was strong" - Joker

But perseverance isn't just about gritting your teeth and pushing through. It's also about finding strength in adversity, as beautifully illustrated by the Joker's words: "And then I smiled once again not because I was happy but because I was strong." This quote reveals a profound truth about the nature of resilience. It's not about always feeling happy or positive in the face of challenges, but about recognizing your own strength in overcoming them.

The smile in this context isn't one of joy, but of acknowledgment - a recognition of one's own resilience and capability. It's about finding a sense of pride and even a glimmer of satisfaction in knowing that you're weathering the storm, that you're proving your strength to yourself. This kind of smile is a powerful tool in your arsenal of perseverance. It's a reminder to yourself that you are stronger than whatever life throws at you.

In your own journey, there will be moments when happiness seems distant, when the weight of your challenges feels overwhelming. In these moments, remember that your strength is not measured by your ability to maintain constant happiness, but by your capacity to endure, to push forward, to smile in the face of adversity not out of joy, but out of an understanding of your own indomitable spirit.

"This too shall pass" – Story of King Solomon and the ring

As we navigate the ups and downs of life, it's crucial to remember the timeless wisdom encapsulated in the biblical phrase,

"This too shall pass." This simple yet profound statement serves as a beacon of hope in our darkest hours and a humbling reminder in our moments of triumph. It speaks to the transient nature of all experiences, both good and bad.

When we're in the midst of a difficult situation, it can feel as though our struggles will last forever. The pain, the frustration, the sense of being overwhelmed - these feelings can cloud our judgment and make us lose sight of the bigger picture. "This too shall pass" reminds us that no matter how dire our current circumstances, they are not permanent. It encourages us to persevere, knowing that better days lie ahead.

Conversely, this phrase also serves as a gentle reminder in times of success and happiness. It encourages us to appreciate and make the most of our good fortune, knowing that life's highs, like its lows, are temporary. This dual nature of the phrase cultivates a balanced perspective on life, fostering resilience in tough times and gratitude in good times.

Incorporating this wisdom into your life doesn't mean adopting a passive attitude towards your circumstances. Rather, it's about maintaining perspective and hope. When faced with challenges, let "This too shall pass" be a mantra that fuels your determination to push through, knowing that your current struggles are not your final destination.

"The higher you get, the harder it gets. That's life" - Tony "Little Duke" Evers, Creed III (2023)

As we climb the ladder of success and personal growth, we often find that new challenges emerge. This reality is perfectly captured in the words of Tony "Little Duke" Evers from Creed III: "The higher you get, the harder it gets. That's life." This quote serves as both a warning and an encouragement, preparing us for the increasing difficulties we'll face as we progress in life while also validating the struggles we encounter along the way.

The path of personal growth and achievement is not a straight line with diminishing resistance. Instead, as we reach new heights in our careers, relationships, or personal development, we often find that the challenges become more complex and demanding. The problems we face at the peak of our profession are often far more intricate than those we encountered at the beginning. The emotional depth required in long-term relationships is greater than in casual acquaintances. The self-reflection and discipline needed to achieve advanced personal growth are more intense than the initial steps of self-improvement.

However, this quote isn't meant to discourage us. Rather, it's a call to continually develop our skills, to grow our capacity for handling complex situations, and to embrace the journey of constant learning and adaptation. It reminds us that the increasing difficulty is a sign of our progress, a testament to how far we've come.

In your own life, as you achieve new levels of success or personal growth, remember that new challenges are not setbacks, but opportunities for further development. Embrace them as signs of your progress and as chances to prove your perseverance and determination once again.

Perseverance and determination are not just about reaching a destination; they're about embracing the journey, with all its ups and downs. They're about finding strength in adversity, maintaining hope in dark times, and continually rising to meet new challenges. As you face your own trials and tribulations, remember the wisdom encapsulated in these quotes. Let them fuel your resolve, remind you of your inner strength, and guide you through the toughest of times.

Your journey is unique, and your challenges are your own. But the spirit of perseverance and determination is universal. It's the force that has driven humanity's greatest achievements and personal triumphs. It resides within you, waiting to be called upon. So, as you move forward in life, carry these words with you. Let them remind you that you can "do this all day," that your smile is a testament to your strength, that all things – good and bad – shall pass, and that each new challenge is a sign of how far you've come.

Embrace your journey with an unbreakable spirit. Persevere. Determine your path. And remember, no matter how difficult it gets, you have the strength within you to rise, to smile, and to keep moving forward. That's the power of perseverance and determination. That's the essence of the unbreakable human spirit.

Chapter 22: The Journey Within - Personal Growth and Transformation

The path of personal growth and transformation is perhaps the most profound journey we undertake in our lives. It's a journey that doesn't always follow a straight line, often leading us through unexpected twists and turns, challenges and triumphs. This internal odyssey shapes who we are, who we become, and how we interact with the world around us. As we explore this theme, we'll delve into three powerful quotes illuminating personal growth and transformation .

"I was never that guy until I was that guy" – Wolverine & Deadpool

Let's begin with Wolverine's poignant reflection: "I was never that guy until I was that guy." This seemingly simple statement carries profound implications about the nature of personal transformation. It speaks to the idea that we all have latent potential within us, waiting to be awakened or developed. Wolverine, a character known for his complex journey from a troubled loner to a heroic figure, embodies the concept of becoming something we never thought possible.

This quote reminds us that transformation often happens gradually, sometimes so subtly that we don't realize we've changed until we look back and see how far we've come. It's about stepping into new roles, embracing new responsibilities, and discovering capabilities we didn't know we possessed. Perhaps you've experienced this in your own life - maybe you never saw yourself as a leader until circumstances pushed you into a leadership role, and you rose to the occasion. Or perhaps you never thought of yourself as resilient until you weathered a significant life challenge and came out stronger on the other side.

The beauty of this perspective is that it opens up infinite possibilities for who we can become. It encourages us to be open to change, to be willing to step out of our comfort zones, and to embrace new aspects of ourselves as they emerge. It's a reminder that our identity is not fixed, but fluid and evolving. We are constantly in the process of becoming, and each new experience, each challenge we face, has the potential to reveal new facets of our character.

"He has to heal from the inside out" - Mary Anne Creed, Creed II (2018)

As we embark on this journey of transformation, it's crucial to understand that true change comes from within. This idea is beautifully captured in Mary Anne Creed's words from the movie Creed II: "He has to heal from the inside out." While spoken in the context of physical recovery, this statement holds profound truth for emotional and personal growth as well.

Too often, we look for external solutions to internal problems. We might seek validation from others, chase material success, or try to change our circumstances without addressing the root causes of our dissatisfaction or pain. But lasting transformation and genuine healing require us to look inward, to confront our fears, insecurities, and past traumas. It's about addressing the core issues that shape our behaviors and mindsets.

Healing from the inside out is not an easy process. It requires courage to face our inner demons, honesty to acknowledge our flaws and mistakes, and patience to allow the healing process to unfold naturally. It might involve revisiting painful memories, questioning long-held beliefs, or letting go of aspects of ourselves that no longer serve us. But this internal work is essential for genuine growth and transformation.

Consider how this applies to your own life. Are there areas where you've been seeking external solutions to internal problems? Perhaps you've been trying to fill an emotional void with material possessions, or attempting to fix a relationship without first addressing your own insecurities or communication issues. Recognizing the need to heal from the inside out can be the first step towards meaningful change.

"You got to the pen now get to the point" - Grandma Mattie

As we navigate this journey of internal healing and transformation, it's easy to get lost in introspection and self-analysis. This is where Grandma Mattie's wise words come into play: "You got to the pen now get to the point." This quote serves as a gentle reminder that while self-reflection is crucial, it must eventually lead to action and concrete change.

In the context of personal growth, "getting to the pen" might represent the process of self-discovery, of exploring our thoughts and feelings, perhaps through journaling, therapy, or deep introspection. It's an essential part of the journey, allowing us to understand ourselves better and identify areas for growth. But Grandma Mattie reminds us that this is not the end goal. We must "get to the point" - we must take what we've learned about ourselves and translate it into meaningful action and change in our lives.

This quote encourages us to avoid the trap of endless introspection without practical application. It's not enough to simply understand our flaws or recognize areas for improvement; we must actively work on changing our behaviors, attitudes, and habits. It's about setting concrete goals for personal growth and taking tangible steps towards achieving them.

For example, if through self-reflection you've realized that fear of failure is holding you back, getting to the point might involve setting small, achievable goals that push you out of your comfort zone. If you've recognized patterns of negative self-talk, it might mean actively practicing positive affirmations or seeking professional help to change these thought patterns. The key is to move from insight to action, from understanding to transformation.

As we weave these three quotes together, we see a comprehensive picture of personal growth and transformation emerge. Wolverine's words remind us of our capacity for change and the potential that lies dormant within us. Mary Anne Creed's insight underscores the importance of internal healing and addressing root causes rather than symptoms. And Grandma Mattie's wisdom calls us to action, urging us to translate our self-knowledge into tangible change.

Your journey of personal growth and transformation is uniquely yours. It will have its own pace, its own challenges, and its own victories. Embrace the process of becoming "that guy" (or gal) you never thought you could be. Allow yourself the time and space to heal from the inside out, addressing the core issues that have held you back. And remember to "get to the point" - to take concrete actions based on your insights and self-discovery.

Remember, transformation is not always comfortable. It often requires us to confront difficult truths about ourselves and to step out of our comfort zones. But it is through this process that we unlock our true potential, heal our deepest wounds, and become the best versions of ourselves.

As you continue on your journey of personal growth and transformation, carry these quotes with you. Let them serve as guideposts, reminding you of the potential within you, the importance of inner healing, and the necessity of taking action. Your transformation is a lifelong journey, filled with opportunities for growth, healing, and self-discovery. Embrace it with open arms, knowing that each step forward is shaping you into the person you are meant to become.

Chapter 23: Purpose and Passion

Purpose and passion are the driving forces that turn an ordinary life into an extraordinary one. The main quote, "Have superpowers and not using them makes you the villain," serves as a powerful reminder that our unique talents and abilities are meant to be utilized, not squandered. This chapter explores how embracing our purpose and pursuing our passions not only fulfills us but also makes a positive impact on the world around us.

"Having superpowers and not using them makes you the villain."

This quote powerfully underscores the idea that neglecting to use one's unique talents and abilities is not just a missed opportunity but a disservice to oneself and others. Everyone possesses "superpowers" in the form of skills, talents, and passions. Failing to utilize these gifts means withholding potential contributions from the world, which can be seen as a form of villainy. Embracing and using one's superpowers leads to personal fulfillment and a positive impact on society.

"You wouldn't be any good to anybody if you didn't do what you love." - Adonis Johnson, Creed II (2018)

Adonis Johnson's words in "Creed II" highlight the importance of passion in achieving excellence and making a meaningful impact. Doing what you love fuels motivation, creativity, and perseverance. When you engage in activities that ignite your passion, you bring your best self to the table, which benefits both you and those around you. This quote emphasizes that pursuing what you love is not selfish; it is essential for being of true value to others.

"Some people want to live forever with no reason to live."-Jim Rohn

This poignant observation reflects the emptiness that comes from living without purpose or passion. Merely existing without a clear reason or direction leads to a hollow life, regardless of its length. True fulfillment comes from having a purpose that gives life meaning and pursuing passions that bring joy and satisfaction. This quote encourages readers to find and embrace their reason for living, ensuring that their time on Earth is meaningful and impactful.

Together, these quotes paint a vivid picture of the significance of purpose and passion in leading a fulfilling life. The main quote challenges readers to recognize and utilize their unique gifts, framing this as a moral imperative. Adonis Johnson's quote underscores the essential connection between passion and being able to contribute meaningfully to others. The final quote serves as a cautionary reminder of the emptiness that results from living without purpose.

Exploring the Superpowers Within

Every individual has unique talents and abilities that can be likened to superpowers. Whether it's a knack for creative problem-solving, a talent for connecting with others, or an aptitude for technical skills, these superpowers are what make us special. However, recognizing these superpowers is only the first step. The true challenge lies in harnessing and applying them in ways that align with our purpose and passions.

This section can delve into exercises and reflections that help readers identify their unique talents and find ways to incorporate them into their daily lives. It could also explore stories of individuals who discovered their superpowers and used them to make a significant impact, serving as inspiration for readers to do the same.

Passion as a Catalyst for Excellence

Passion is the fuel that drives us to excel in what we do. When we engage in activities that we are passionate about, we are more likely to invest time, effort, and creativity, leading to higher levels of achievement and satisfaction. This section can discuss how finding and following one's passions can lead to a more fulfilling life and greater contributions to the world.

Incorporating anecdotes from successful individuals who have pursued their passions despite challenges can provide motivational examples. Additionally, offering practical tips for discovering and nurturing one's passions can help readers take actionable steps towards a more passionate and purpose-driven life.

The Perils of a Passionless Life

Living without purpose or passion leads to a sense of emptiness and dissatisfaction. This section can explore the dangers of a passionless life, including the mental and emotional toll it takes. It can discuss how finding a purpose provides direction and meaning, transforming life from mere existence into a fulfilling journey.

Sharing stories of individuals who struggled with a lack of purpose and how they overcame it can provide hope and guidance. This section can also include exercises for self-reflection and goal-setting to help readers identify and pursue their own purpose and passions.

Practical Steps to Embrace Purpose and Passion

The final section can offer practical advice for integrating purpose and passion into daily life. This can include strategies for setting meaningful goals, creating a vision board, and developing habits that align with one's purpose. It can also discuss the importance of surrounding oneself with supportive and like-minded individuals who encourage and inspire the pursuit of passions.

Chapter 24: Self-Reflection and Inner Peace

Self-reflection and inner peace are vital components of a fulfilling and balanced life. This chapter delves into the importance of introspection, understanding oneself, and finding tranquility amidst life's challenges. The main quote, "I've been losing friends and finding peace" by Drake, sets the tone for exploring the journey of self-discovery and the pursuit of inner calm.

"I've been losing friends and finding peace." - Drake

Drake's quote highlights the often difficult yet necessary process of prioritizing inner peace over external relationships. It speaks to the reality that personal growth and self-reflection can sometimes lead to losing connections that no longer serve our well-being. This journey toward peace may involve making tough decisions, but it ultimately leads to a more authentic and serene life. Embracing self-reflection and inner peace often means reassessing relationships and environments, letting go of what causes turmoil, and seeking what nurtures the soul.

"Do not build a case against yourself." - Unknown

This quote emphasizes the importance of self-compassion and positive self-talk. Often, individuals are their harshest critics, constantly judging themselves and building a negative narrative. This detrimental behavior can hinder personal growth and inner peace. By recognizing this tendency and actively working against it, one can cultivate a more supportive and understanding relationship with oneself. Self-reflection should be a tool for growth, not self-condemnation.

"As long as you're talking, you're not listening." - Rocky Balboa, Creed (2015)

Rocky Balboa's wisdom underscores the value of listening, both to oneself and to others. In the context of self-reflection, it means quieting the constant internal chatter to truly hear one's inner voice and understand one's thoughts and emotions. This practice fosters a deeper connection with oneself and promotes inner peace. Additionally, listening actively to others can improve relationships and provide new perspectives, further enriching one's journey toward inner tranquility.

Together, these quotes offer a comprehensive guide to achieving self-reflection and inner peace. Drake's quote sets the stage by highlighting the sometimes painful but necessary process of prioritizing peace over turbulent relationships. The unknown quote encourages self-compassion and the rejection of negative self-judgment, while Rocky Balboa's advice emphasizes the importance of listening and introspection.

Prioritizing Inner Peace Over External Validation

Drake's quote underscores the reality that the pursuit of inner peace can lead to losing friends who are not aligned with one's journey. This section can discuss the importance of prioritizing mental and emotional well-being over external validation and the fear of losing relationships. It can offer strategies for navigating these difficult transitions and finding peace amidst change.

Stories of individuals who made tough choices to prioritize their peace and the positive outcomes that followed can provide inspiration and guidance. This section can also explore how to build new, healthier relationships that support personal growth and tranquility.

The Importance of Self-Compassion

The quote, "Do not build a case against yourself," emphasizes the need for self-compassion. This section can delve into the negative effects of self-criticism and the importance of cultivating a supportive inner dialogue. It can offer practical tips for developing self-compassion, such as mindfulness exercises, affirmations, and self-care routines.

By sharing anecdotes and exercises that promote self-compassion, readers can learn to treat themselves with the kindness and understanding they deserve, fostering a more peaceful and harmonious inner life.

The Art of Listening and Introspection

Rocky Balboa's quote highlights the importance of listening as a crucial aspect of self-reflection. This section can explore the benefits of active listening, both to oneself and to others. It can provide techniques for quieting the mind, such as meditation, journaling, and mindfulness practices, to enhance self-awareness and introspection.

Additionally, this section can discuss the importance of listening to others to gain new perspectives and build deeper connections. By fostering a habit of active listening, readers can enhance their self-reflection practices and cultivate inner peace.

Practical Steps to Achieve Self-Reflection and Inner Peace

The final section can offer practical advice for integrating self-reflection and inner peace into daily life. This can include creating a regular practice of meditation or journaling, setting boundaries to protect one's peace, and seeking out environments and relationships that nurture well-being.

By providing actionable steps and practical guidance, this section ensures that readers have the tools they need to embark on their journey of self-discovery and inner tranquility. It can also encourage readers to be patient and compassionate with themselves as they navigate this process.

Chapter 25: Dreams and Ambition

Dreams and ambition are the driving forces that propel individuals toward achieving their highest potential. This chapter explores the significance of dreams, the challenges that can threaten their survival, and the relentless pursuit of ambition. The main quote, "Dreams die with suffering" by the Last Prophet, sets the stage for a deep dive into how dreams can be nurtured and sustained through resilience and hard work.

"Dreams die with suffering." - Last Prophet,Deepak Chopra

The Last Prophet's quote, "Dreams die with suffering," poignantly captures the fragile nature of dreams. Suffering, in this context, can represent a range of challenges, from personal hardships to external obstacles. The essence of the quote lies in the understanding that suffering has the potential to extinguish dreams if not confronted with resilience and determination. It serves as a reminder that nurturing dreams requires perseverance, even in the face of adversity.

"When you have dreams so small they become, those goals become a nuisance." - Jim Rohn

Jim Rohn's quote highlights the importance of dreaming big. Small dreams can become insignificant and easily disregarded, turning into mere distractions rather than meaningful pursuits. This quote encourages individuals to set ambitious goals that challenge and inspire them. The essence of ambition lies in daring to dream big and pursuing those dreams with unwavering commitment. Rohn's perspective urges readers to avoid settling for mediocrity and instead aim for greatness.

"Magic doesn't make it work, how we work makes it magic." - Lee Cockerell

Lee Cockerell's quote emphasizes the role of hard work in achieving dreams. There is no magical formula for success; instead, it is the dedication and effort put into the pursuit of dreams that create the magic. This quote serves as a powerful reminder that dreams require not just passion but also consistent and disciplined action. It dismantles the myth of overnight success and underscores the importance of persistence and hard work.

Together, these quotes offer a comprehensive view of dreams and ambition. The Last Prophet's quote sets the foundation by acknowledging the vulnerability of dreams in the face of suffering. Jim Rohn's quote inspires readers to dream big, while Lee Cockerell's quote underscores the necessity of hard work in turning dreams into reality.

Nurturing Dreams Amidst Adversity

The main quote by the Last Prophet serves as a starting point for discussing the challenges that can threaten dreams. This section can explore various forms of suffering, such as self-doubt, failure, and external obstacles, and how they can potentially derail dreams. By acknowledging these challenges, readers can prepare to face them with resilience.

Stories of individuals who have faced significant hardships but continued to pursue their dreams can provide inspiration and practical insights. This section can also offer strategies for maintaining motivation and resilience, such as setting short-term goals, seeking support from mentors and peers, and practicing self-care.

The Power of Big Dreams

Jim Rohn's quote highlights the importance of setting ambitious goals. This section can delve into the psychology of dreaming big and how it influences motivation and achievement. It can discuss the dangers of setting goals that are too small and easily achievable, leading to complacency and a lack of fulfillment.

By exploring the concept of SMART goals (Specific, Measurable, Achievable, Relevant, Time-bound), readers can learn how to set challenging yet attainable objectives that push them toward their ultimate dreams. Real-life examples of successful individuals who dared to dream big and achieved remarkable feats can further illustrate the power of ambitious goals.

The Role of Hard Work

Lee Cockerell's quote emphasizes that dreams require consistent effort and dedication. This section can explore the myth of overnight success and highlight the importance of perseverance and hard work in achieving dreams. It can provide practical advice on developing a strong work ethic, such as time management, setting priorities, and maintaining focus.

The section can also address the importance of resilience in the face of setbacks. By learning to view failures as opportunities for growth and staying committed to their goals, readers can develop the mindset necessary to turn their dreams into reality.

Practical Steps to Pursue Dreams and Ambition

The final section can offer actionable advice for readers to integrate dreams and ambition into their daily lives. This can include creating a vision board to visualize their goals, breaking down large dreams into manageable steps, and celebrating small victories along the way.

By providing tools and techniques for staying motivated and focused, this section ensures that readers are equipped to pursue their dreams with determination and resilience. Encouraging readers to surround themselves with supportive and like-minded individuals can further enhance their journey toward achieving their dreams.

Chapter 26: Life Lessons and Wisdom

Life is a journey filled with lessons and wisdom that shape who we are and how we navigate the world. This chapter explores profound insights and truths that can guide us through life's challenges and triumphs. The main quote, "We all need a Judas in our life" by Grandma Mattie, sets the stage for a discussion on the importance of adversaries, the inevitability of time, and the hidden costs of favors.

"We all need a Judas in our life." - Grandma Mattie

Grandma Mattie's quote, "We all need a Judas in our life," reflects the idea that adversaries or betrayers play a crucial role in our personal growth and development. Just as Judas' betrayal was pivotal in the story of Jesus, adversities and challenges often propel us to greater heights. These individuals or situations push us to reevaluate our paths, strengthen our resolve, and ultimately become better versions of ourselves. This perspective encourages readers to view challenges not as setbacks but as necessary catalysts for growth.

"Time takes everybody out." - Rocky Balboa, Creed (2015)

Rocky Balboa's statement from "Creed" underscores the inevitability of time and its impact on our lives. Time is the great equalizer; it affects everyone, regardless of status or strength. This quote serves as a reminder of our mortality and the importance of making the most of the time we have. It urges readers to live with urgency and intention, valuing each moment and making choices that reflect their true priorities and values.

"Be careful to ask for, or accept a favor, they always cost more." - Nathan Shafer

Nathan Shafer's quote highlights the often-overlooked costs of favors. While favors might seem like simple acts of kindness, they can come with hidden strings attached. This wisdom advises caution in both seeking and accepting favors, as they can lead to obligations and expectations that may outweigh the initial benefit. It encourages readers to consider the long-term implications of their actions and to strive for independence and self-reliance.

These quotes collectively provide a rich tapestry of life lessons and wisdom. Grandma Mattie's quote teaches the value of adversaries, Rocky Balboa's quote underscores the importance of time, and Nathan Shafer's quote offers a cautionary tale about favors.

The Value of Adversaries

The main quote by Grandma Mattie opens a discussion on the role of adversaries and challenges in our lives. This section can explore how difficult people and situations often bring out our best qualities, forcing us to adapt, grow, and overcome. By embracing adversity as a necessary part of life, readers can develop resilience and a growth mindset.

Stories of historical figures, entrepreneurs, and everyday individuals who faced significant challenges but emerged stronger can provide concrete examples. This section can also offer strategies for dealing with difficult people and situations, such as maintaining a positive attitude, seeking lessons in adversity, and using challenges as motivation.

The Inevitability of Time

Rocky Balboa's quote emphasizes the importance of recognizing the passage of time and its impact on our lives. This section can delve into the concept of time management and the significance of living a life aligned with one's values and goals. It can discuss the fleeting nature of time and the importance of making every moment count.

Readers can be encouraged to reflect on their life choices and prioritize activities that bring them fulfillment and joy. Practical advice on setting goals, creating a balanced life, and avoiding procrastination can help readers make the most of their time.

The Hidden Costs of Favors

Nathan Shafer's quote provides a cautionary perspective on the true cost of favors. This section can explore the dynamics of giving and receiving favors, including the potential for dependency and unspoken obligations. It can discuss the importance of setting boundaries and being mindful of the implications of favors.

By encouraging readers to seek independence and self-reliance, this section helps them understand the value of maintaining control over their lives. It can offer advice on how to graciously decline favors and seek mutual, balanced relationships where both parties benefit equally.

Practical Steps for Applying Life Lessons

The final section can provide actionable steps for readers to integrate these life lessons into their daily lives. This can include tips for developing resilience, managing time effectively, and navigating the complexities of favors and obligations. By offering practical advice, this section ensures that readers are equipped to apply the wisdom and insights gained from the chapter.

Encouraging readers to reflect on their experiences and extract valuable lessons can help them grow and evolve. Journaling, seeking mentorship, and engaging in self-improvement activities can further support their journey toward wisdom and personal growth.

Chapter 27: Personal Responsibility and Action

Taking personal responsibility is essential for living a fulfilling and successful life. This chapter delves into the importance of owning one's actions, intentions, and responses to life's circumstances. The main quote, "Don't lie about me and I won't tell truths about you" by Kendrick Lamar, sets the stage for an exploration of integrity, intention, and fear of change.

"Don't lie about me and I won't tell truths about you." - Kendrick Lamar

Kendrick Lamar's quote emphasizes the importance of honesty and integrity in interpersonal relationships. It suggests a reciprocal agreement where mutual respect and truthfulness are maintained. This quote encourages readers to reflect on their own actions and the impact of dishonesty, while also highlighting the value of maintaining integrity in all interactions. By living truthfully, individuals can foster trust and respect in their relationships, creating a foundation for positive and meaningful connections.

"Intention is an opportunity for excuse making." - Jim Rohn

Jim Rohn's quote suggests that intentions alone are insufficient; they must be accompanied by action. Good intentions without follow-through can lead to excuses and inaction. This quote urges readers to transform their intentions into concrete actions, emphasizing the importance of accountability and discipline. By taking decisive steps toward their goals, individuals can overcome procrastination and achieve tangible results.

"Are you afraid to lose a job you absolutely hate?" - Jim Rohn

Another powerful insight from Jim Rohn, this quote challenges readers to confront their fears and question the value of holding onto unfulfilling situations. It prompts individuals to assess whether their fear of change is preventing them from pursuing their true passions and potential. By overcoming fear and embracing change, readers can find greater satisfaction and purpose in their lives.

These quotes collectively underscore the importance of personal responsibility, integrity, and action. Kendrick Lamar's quote highlights the need for honesty, Jim Rohn's quotes emphasize the necessity of transforming intentions into actions and overcoming fear.

Honesty and Integrity in Relationships

Kendrick Lamar's quote sets the tone for a discussion on the significance of honesty and integrity in personal and professional relationships. This section can explore the consequences of dishonesty and the benefits of maintaining a truthful and transparent approach. Readers can be encouraged to reflect on their own behaviors and make a conscious effort to uphold integrity in all their interactions.

Real-life examples and stories of individuals who have experienced the repercussions of dishonesty, as well as those who have thrived through maintaining integrity, can provide valuable insights. Practical advice on fostering trust and respect in relationships can further guide readers toward building strong and healthy connections.

Transforming Intentions into Actions

Jim Rohn's quote about intentions serves as a reminder that good intentions must be backed by action to create meaningful change. This section can delve into the reasons why people often fail to act on their intentions and provide strategies to overcome these barriers. By understanding the psychology of procrastination and the importance of discipline, readers can learn how to turn their intentions into concrete actions.

Practical steps such as setting clear goals, creating actionable plans, and holding oneself accountable can help readers bridge the gap between intention and action. Stories of individuals who have successfully transformed their intentions into achievements can inspire and motivate readers to take decisive steps toward their goals.

Overcoming Fear and Embracing Change

Jim Rohn's second quote challenges readers to confront their fears, particularly the fear of losing a job or situation they dislike. This section can explore the concept of fear and how it often prevents individuals from pursuing their true passions and potential. By examining the psychology of fear and the comfort zone, readers can learn to recognize and overcome their limiting beliefs.

Encouraging readers to take calculated risks and embrace change can lead to greater fulfillment and success. Practical advice on managing fear, building confidence, and taking proactive steps toward change can empower readers to leave unfulfilling situations and pursue their dreams.

Practical Steps for Taking Personal Responsibility

The final section can provide actionable steps for readers to take personal responsibility and implement the insights gained from the chapter. This can include tips for maintaining integrity, transforming intentions into actions, and overcoming fear. By offering practical advice, this section ensures that readers are equipped to apply the principles of personal responsibility in their daily lives.

Encouraging readers to set personal goals, track their progress, and seek support from mentors or accountability partners can help them stay on track. Reflecting on their experiences and celebrating their achievements can further reinforce the importance of personal responsibility and action.

Chapter: Embracing Your Journey

As we draw to a close, it's essential to reflect on the journey we've undertaken through this book. The chapters have traversed the landscapes of resilience, vision, purpose, relationships, personal responsibility, and more. We've drawn inspiration from powerful quotes and profound wisdom, each serving as a beacon to guide us through the complexities of life.

The essence of this book is encapsulated in the idea that our lives are a mosaic of choices, actions, and reflections. It is through these elements that we shape our destinies and uncover our true selves. Each chapter has aimed to provide not just insights, but practical tools to empower you to face life's challenges, embrace new beginnings, and cultivate resilience.

Embracing Change and Growth

From the initial pages, we explored how to embrace new beginnings. Alexander Graham Bell's wisdom on closed doors and new opportunities taught us the importance of looking forward rather than dwelling on what has been lost. As we move forward, let this principle guide you in finding new paths and possibilities even when faced with setbacks.

The chapters on resilience and personal growth emphasized that our greatest strength lies in our ability to rise every time we fall. Nelson Mandela's words and the wisdom of the ancients remind us that personal development is a continuous journey, marked by our responses to challenges and our capacity to grow from them.

The Power of Action and Vision

Vision without execution is indeed mere hallucination, as we learned. Our exploration into vision and action has highlighted the need for practical steps and relentless effort. Jay-Z's testament to persistence and Edison's call to hustle underscore the importance of transforming vision into reality. As you move forward, remember that every step taken toward your goals is a victory in itself.

In embracing your purpose and passion, we've discussed how to recognize and utilize your unique strengths and passions. The exploration of purpose teaches us that fulfillment comes from aligning our actions with what we truly care about. Your superpowers, when actively used, become a force for good, propelling you toward a life of meaning and impact.

Nurturing Relationships and Inner Peace

The chapters on relationships and inner peace remind us of the value of authentic connections and self-awareness. The insights from Deadpool, Steve Rogers, and Dr. Strange on relationships emphasize that true bonds are built on mutual respect and understanding. At the same time, Drake's reflection on peace and the wisdom of Grandma Mattie on self-doubt and fear provide valuable lessons on maintaining inner calm amidst external chaos.

Remember, personal responsibility is the cornerstone of meaningful change. Kendrick Lamar's emphasis on honesty and Jim Rohn's insights into intention and fear challenge us to take ownership of our actions and decisions. By embracing these principles, you are empowered to create a life that is authentic, purposeful, and fulfilling.

Living Your Best Life

As we conclude this journey, it is crucial to integrate the lessons learned into your daily life. Embrace the power of action, maintain your integrity, and transform your intentions into tangible results. Face life's challenges with courage and resilience, and let your relationships and purpose guide you toward a life of true fulfillment.

Your story is continuously unfolding. Each day presents a new opportunity to apply the insights gained and to make choices that align with your values and goals. By embracing the principles discussed in this book, you are well-equipped to navigate the complexities of life with confidence and clarity.

In the end, remember that the path to greatness is not a straight line but a series of twists and turns, victories and setbacks. Embrace each moment, learn from every experience, and continue to move forward with purpose and passion. Your journey is uniquely yours, and with each step, you have the power to shape your destiny and illuminate your greatness.

Thank you for joining me on this exploration of resilience, vision, purpose, and action. May the lessons and insights gained serve as a guiding light on your path to a life of fulfillment and impact. Your journey begins now—embrace it with courage, integrity, and unwavering commitment.

About the Author

Ray Shoulders is a dedicated man of God, husband, father, writer, and motivational speaker with a passion for empowering others to overcome adversity. Drawing from personal experiences and the wisdom of his mother and grandmother, Ray's work focuses on resilience, persistence, and personal growth. He aims to inspire readers to harness their inner strength and embrace the power of comebacks in their own lives.